SECURITY, History of the Night-Time Economy

SECURITY, HISTORY OF THE NIGHT-TIME ECONOMY

First edition. December 8, 2024.

ISBN: 979-8230565055

Written by Antonio Templar.

Dedication

This book is dedicated to the countless men and women who have served, and continue to serve, as the unsung guardians of the night. Their dedication, often underappreciated and frequently tested, ensures the safety and enjoyment of millions. This work is a testament to their resilience, professionalism, and the enduring bonds of camaraderie forged within the challenging environment of the security industry. It is also dedicated to those whose lives have been touched by the work of these professionals – the patrons, the venue owners, and the communities they protect. May this book serve as a tribute to their often-overlooked contributions to our society's vibrant, yet complex, night-time culture, and offer a glimpse into the rich history and evolving role of those who ensure its continued safety and prosperity. To my fellow door supervisors, past and present: your stories are the heart of this narrative. Thank you for sharing your experiences, and for your unwavering

commitment to safeguarding the night.

Preface

For years, the individuals who secure our night-time

economy have remained largely unseen, their contributions often overlooked in the broader societal narrative. This book aims to rectify that oversight. It seeks to illuminate the rich and multifaceted history of security within the night-time entertainment industry, from its humble beginnings to its current sophisticated state, regulated by the Security Industry Authority (SIA). More than just a historical account, this work explores the unique and often challenging culture that defines the security profession. It delves into the camaraderie, the shared experiences, and the unwavering commitment to duty that unite those who patrol the pubs, clubs, and events that define our nocturnal landscape.

Through a blend of historical analysis, personal accounts, and insightful observations, this book offers a

comprehensive exploration of the evolution of security training, the integration of technology, and the enduring impact of security professionals on public safety. The stories shared within these pages—drawn from extensive research, interviews, and personal experiences—reveal not only the historical context but also the human element at the core of this crucial industry. It is a journey into a world often shrouded in shadows, but one that holds within it stories of courage, resilience, and a steadfast dedication to safeguarding our communities. I hope this book provides a newfound appreciation for the vital role these individuals play in the fabric of our society.

Introduction

The night-time economy: a vibrant tapestry woven with threads of entertainment, social interaction, and economic activity. But beneath the surface of this lively landscape lies a crucial element often unseen, yet essential to its very existence: security. This book unravels the fascinating history of security within this dynamic environment, tracing its evolution from the informal methods of yesteryear to the highly regulated profession of today. We journey from the dimly lit pubs and boisterous dance halls of the past, where crowd control was often a matter of brute strength and

improvisation, to the technologically advanced venues of the present, monitored by sophisticated surveillance systems and staffed by SIA-licensed professionals. We will examine the crucial role legislation, such as the establishment of the SIA, played in shaping the industry, demanding higher standards of training and accountability. But this is not merely a chronicle of regulation and technological advancement. It is also a deeply human story. It is about the brotherhood and shared responsibilities that bind security personnel together, the challenges they face daily, and the resilience they display in the face of adversity. Through personal accounts and historical analysis, we will uncover the cultural landscape of the profession, examining the unique camaraderie, the psychological pressures, and the often-overlooked contributions of those who stand as guardians of the night. From the early days of rudimentary training methods to the sophisticated training regimens of today, we explore the evolution of professional development, highlighting the constant adaptation needed to meet the ever-changing demands of a complex and often dangerous industry. Prepare to enter a world rarely glimpsed, a world where the stories of courage, dedication, and the unwavering commitment to safety are finally brought to light.

Early Forms of Crowd Control and Venue Security

Before the advent of formal security regulations and the rise of the professional door supervisor, the safety and order of pubs and entertainment venues relied heavily on informal, often haphazard, methods. The role of maintaining order frequently fell to the publican themselves, a figure who was simultaneously businessman, host, and, by necessity, peacekeeper. In smaller establishments, the publican's authority, often bolstered by their personal strength and local reputation, was the primary deterrent against trouble. Larger establishments might employ a "bouncer," a term evocative of the rudimentary nature of the role. These individuals, often recruited for their size and perceived toughness, were essentially hired muscle, lacking any formal training or standardized approach to conflict management. Their methods were often brutal and reactive, focused on ejecting disruptive patrons with little regard for de-escalation or finesse.

The social context of this era significantly shaped these practices. Urban centers, particularly during periods of rapid industrialization and social change, often witnessed a surge in public disorder and violence. Pubs and entertainment venues, hubs of social activity, frequently became focal points for these tensions. Alcohol played a significant role, fueling aggression and exacerbating existing social conflicts.

The police presence in these areas was often limited,

especially in the later hours of the night, leaving publicans and their informal security personnel to manage disturbances largely on their own. This created an environment where violence and public disorder were relatively commonplace, accepted, perhaps even expected, to a degree shocking by today's standards.

The lack of formal regulation contributed to a chaotic and often dangerous environment. There were no standardized training programs, no licensing requirements, and no regulatory bodies overseeing the practices of pub security personnel. This lack of oversight meant that the competence and behavior of these individuals varied dramatically. Some might have possessed a natural aptitude for conflict resolution and crowd management, while others resorted to intimidation, brutality, and even unlawful actions with impunity. This lack of accountability made the industry prone to abuse, contributing to the often-violent and

unpredictable nature of nightlife.

Historical accounts paint a vivid picture of this era.

Newspaper reports from the late 19th and early 20th

centuries regularly featured accounts of pub brawls, often involving multiple participants, significant injuries, and even fatalities. These reports reveal a culture of violence deeply ingrained within certain sectors of society, where physical confrontations were a relatively common occurrence in public spaces. The descriptions often highlight the chaotic nature of these events, with patrons spilling out onto the streets, engaging in violent clashes, and police struggling to restore order. While the accounts are frequently sensationalized, the underlying reality was that the night-time economy was a much more physically dangerous place than it is today.

The methods of crowd control in this era were rudimentary at best. Physical strength and intimidation were the primary tools employed, and strategic crowd management techniques were largely non-existent. Large groups of patrons were managed primarily through a display of force, often involving threats, shoving, and physical ejection of disruptive individuals. Simple, often poorly maintained physical barriers, such as ropes or wooden stanchions, were used to create boundaries, but these provided minimal

protection against determined individuals or large-scale disturbances. The lack of effective communication systems further hampered response times, often resulting in escalating conflicts. The idea of "de-escalation," a central tenet of modern security training, was largely unknown, with the response to trouble typically involving immediate and often excessive force.

The role of the publican in maintaining order varied greatly depending on the size and location of the establishment, and their own personality. Some publicans were known for their ability to create a welcoming and orderly environment, using their personal charisma and authority to prevent trouble.

They would often know their regular customers well and could often defuse potential conflicts before they escalated. However, others might have been less skilled or less inclined to intervene, leading to a more volatile atmosphere. The publican's attitude toward conflict and their willingness to engage with potentially disruptive patrons played a significant role in shaping the overall security environment of their establishment.

The emergence of dedicated bouncers brought a degree of specialization to the role of maintaining order, although this was far from consistent or regulated. These individuals were often recruited based on their physical attributes, with little or no consideration given to their temperament, conflict resolution skills, or understanding of legal limitations. This meant that many bouncers were as likely to exacerbate problems as resolve them. Their methods often bordered on or crossed into the realm of vigilantism, reflecting the lawless nature of the times and the lack of formal oversight.

Anecdotal evidence suggests many bouncers employed heavy-handed tactics, and violent encounters were frequent.

The lack of training and regulation led to inconsistencies in their behaviour and performance, with some performing effectively and others escalating conflicts. These inconsistencies would eventually be recognised as a significant problem requiring formal regulation.

The informal and unregulated nature of early security

practices in the night-time economy created a unique, and often perilous, environment. While the publicans and

bouncers of this era played a crucial role in maintaining a semblance of order, their methods were largely reactive, lacking the sophistication and professional training of

modern security personnel. This period laid bare the urgent need for formal regulation, standardized training, and a greater understanding of effective crowd management and conflict resolution techniques. The legacy of this era, however, continues to inform the development of security practices and regulations today, highlighting the importance of balancing firmness with effective de-escalation techniques and adherence to legal standards. The evolution from informal, often violent, crowd control to the regulated profession of today is a testament to the changing social landscape and the importance of ensuring public safety within the night-time economy. The shift reflects a growing societal awareness of the importance of professionalism, accountability, and the responsible use of power. The stories of early security practices stand as a stark reminder of the progress that has been made, and a cautionary tale against complacency.

The Rise of Professionalism and the Birth of the Door Supervisor

The shift towards professionalization in the security industry wasn't a sudden revolution but rather a gradual evolution, driven by a confluence of factors. The increasing urbanization of the late 20th century played a significant role. As cities swelled with populations migrating from rural areas and smaller towns, the demands on existing, informal security measures became unsustainable. Larger crowds congregated in pubs, clubs, and entertainment venues, increasing the likelihood of incidents requiring more sophisticated crowd management and conflict resolution skills than a burly bouncer could provide. The sheer scale of these gatherings outstripped the capacity of pub owners and their informal security arrangements.

Furthermore, societal changes contributed significantly to this transition. The post-war boom and the rise of youth culture brought with it new forms of social interaction and, inevitably, new challenges for maintaining order. The emergence of rock and roll music, for instance, led to larger, more energetic crowds, requiring security personnel capable of managing potentially volatile situations. Traditional methods of intimidation were increasingly ineffective against a more assertive and less deferential younger generation.

This necessitated a move away from brute force towards more nuanced approaches, emphasizing de-escalation techniques and an understanding of crowd psychology.

The legal landscape also played its part. Increased awareness of civil liberties and the potential for liability in cases of excessive force pushed venue owners and managers towards more regulated security practices. The risk of legal repercussions, coupled with the rising cost of insurance claims stemming from incidents involving untrained security personnel, incentivized a move towards professionalism. Insurance companies, recognizing the growing risk, began to demand higher standards of security provision from the venues they insured, leading to a cascade effect across the industry.

The initial steps towards professionalism involved the establishment of small, often family-run, security firms.

These firms, while still operating within a largely

unregulated environment, represented a significant step forward from the individual bouncer model. They offered a level of consistency and accountability that was previously lacking. Employing several security personnel rather than just one allowed for more effective crowd management and better response times in case of incidents. These early firms frequently adopted rudimentary training programs, focusing on basic conflict resolution techniques, communication skills, and, importantly, legal awareness. While these training programs were far from the rigorous standards set by today's Security Industry Authority (SIA), they

represented a crucial departure from the wholly unregulated, largely untrained security staff of previous eras.

The evolution of training was not uniform across the board, varying significantly based on geographic location, the type of venue, and the resources available to the individual security firms. In some areas, local police forces played a crucial role in providing basic training to security personnel, offering workshops on de-escalation tactics and legal limitations. Other firms developed their own in-house training programs, drawing on the experience of their senior staff members. These programs often involved practical exercises, role-playing scenarios, and instruction on identifying and responding to different types of threats.

One significant development was the standardization of security procedures within specific venues or districts.

Larger venues, particularly those attracting large crowds, began to implement more structured security protocols, creating detailed guidelines on crowd control, entry and exit procedures, and incident reporting. These protocols often involved the use of radios and communication systems, allowing security personnel to coordinate their actions more effectively. This internal standardization demonstrated a significant shift in thinking, moving away from reactive, individual responses towards a proactive, coordinated

approach to security management.

The emergence of professional security firms also marked the beginning of the formalization of roles within the security industry. The term "door supervisor," while not yet legally codified, began to appear more frequently in job advertisements and internal security documentation. This helped to establish a clearer definition of the role and its responsibilities. Door supervisors were no longer simply muscle for hire but increasingly recognized as individuals with specialized skills and responsibilities, playing a pivotal role in ensuring the safety and security of patrons and staff within the venue.

The early days of professionalized security also witnessed the emergence of specialized equipment. The use of walkie-talkies and metal detectors, while still rudimentary compared to today's technology, represented a significant step forward.

These tools improved communication and allowed for a more proactive approach to security, enabling early detection of potential threats and more efficient coordination between security staff. The adoption of these technologies, even in their early forms, underlined the growing professionalization of the industry and the growing acknowledgement of its significance in ensuring public safety.

The transition from informal to formal security arrangements was not without its challenges. The lack of comprehensive regulation meant that standards varied widely, and inconsistencies in training and procedures were common.

The industry was often characterized by a lack of

transparency and accountability, which sometimes led to abuses of power. This underscored the need for a robust regulatory framework, something which would only emerge later.

Yet, this period marked a crucial turning point. The

increasing professionalism of the security industry, fueled by urbanization, changing social dynamics, and the evolving legal landscape, laid the groundwork for the highly regulated, professionally trained workforce that we see today. The early security firms, though often small and operating with limited resources, were pioneers, laying the foundation for a profession dedicated to ensuring the safety and security of the night-time economy, a profession that would continue to evolve and adapt to meet the constantly changing challenges of the 21st century. The stories of these early pioneers, often unsung and unrecorded, represent a vital piece of the larger puzzle in understanding the development of the security industry and its place within the broader socio-economic context of the 20th century. Their efforts, however imperfect, represent the first steps on the path towards the standardized and regulated industry that exists today, a journey marked by significant progress and continuous adaptation. The ongoing evolution of the industry highlights the dynamic interplay between technological advancement, social change, and the ever-present need to maintain safety and order within the vibrant, and sometimes volatile, world of the night-time economy. The foundation laid by these early pioneers remains a cornerstone of the industry's success. The challenges they faced and the solutions they devised continue to inform and shape the future of night-time security, providing invaluable lessons for those who continue to work within this challenging but crucial profession. The legacy of this era serves as a potent reminder of the importance of continuous professional development and the ongoing need for adaptation and improvement. The journey from rudimentary "bouncers" to the highly trained and regulated door supervisors of today represents a remarkable transformation, a story woven with threads of social change, technological advancement, and a persistent dedication to public safety.

The Impact of Legislation and Regulation on the Industry

The increasing professionalism of the security industry, as outlined in the previous section, wasn't solely a product of societal shifts and the inherent demands of a burgeoning night-time economy. A critical catalyst for this transformation was the intervention of the law, a force that fundamentally reshaped the industry's landscape and the very nature of its practitioners. The introduction of legislation and regulation, initially piecemeal and reactive, eventually coalesced into a comprehensive framework that standardized training, licensing, and operational practices, raising the bar for professionalism and accountability. This legal evolution didn't occur in a vacuum; it was a response to societal

pressures, public safety concerns, and the escalating

complexity of the venues it sought to protect.

The early years of the night-time economy were largely unregulated. Pubs and clubs employed bouncers, often individuals with a reputation for physical strength and

intimidation, operating with minimal oversight and training.

Their methods, while sometimes effective in deterring trouble, frequently lacked the necessary skills to de-escalate conflicts or respond appropriately to diverse situations. Incidents of excessive force, discrimination, and inadequate crowd management were commonplace, leading to public outcry and calls for reform. This period of largely unregulated activity laid the groundwork for a future where regulation became necessary not only to improve safety, but to protect the security personnel themselves from potential liability.

The initial legislative interventions were often focused on specific aspects of security operations, addressing pressing concerns as they arose. For example, early legislation might have focused on the licensing of premises serving alcohol, imposing obligations on venue owners to ensure adequate security measures were in place. These early regulations often lacked the specificity and comprehensive approach that would later characterize the industry's regulatory framework.

The enforcement of these initial regulations was often

inconsistent, varying significantly across different

geographical areas, depending on local policing priorities and the resources available. This inconsistency highlighted the need for a more centralized and standardized approach, a need that would eventually be fulfilled by the creation of specialized regulatory bodies.

The shift towards a more formalized approach to security regulation gained momentum throughout the latter half of the 20th century. Several factors contributed to this

development. Increasing public awareness of the problems associated with inadequate security practices, fuelled by media coverage of incidents and accidents, created pressure on lawmakers to intervene. The growing complexity of the night-time economy, with larger venues and more diverse crowds, also necessitated a more sophisticated and professional approach to security management. Additionally, the growing recognition of the potential liability faced by venue owners and security personnel for incidents occurring on their premises spurred a demand for improved training and standardized operational procedures.

This growing pressure for reform culminated in the creation of the Security Industry Authority (SIA) in the United Kingdom, a landmark event that fundamentally reshaped the security industry. The SIA's establishment marked a decisive shift from a largely unregulated environment to a profession governed by stringent licensing and training requirements.

The SIA's role went beyond simply issuing licenses; it

established a comprehensive framework for regulating all aspects of the private security industry, including door

supervisors. This included setting minimum training

standards, conducting background checks on applicants, and establishing a disciplinary process for dealing with

misconduct. The introduction of the SIA license, and

subsequent associated regulations, ensured that only

individuals who had undergone appropriate training and vetting were permitted to work in regulated security roles.

The impact of the SIA's regulations on the security industry was profound and multifaceted. It raised the professional standards within the sector, leading to a more skilled and responsible workforce. The introduction of mandatory training programs significantly improved the ability of security personnel to handle challenging situations, de-escalate conflicts, and provide effective crowd management. The training curricula incorporated elements such as conflict resolution, communication skills, legal awareness, and first aid, equipping security personnel with the tools and

knowledge to perform their duties effectively and safely.

This shift in training methodologies emphasized de-escalation and conflict resolution over purely physical control, reflecting a wider societal shift toward less confrontational approaches to conflict management.

Furthermore, the SIA's licensing scheme provided a

mechanism for identifying and removing unsuitable

individuals from the industry. The rigorous background checks conducted as part of the licensing process helped to prevent individuals with criminal records or a history of violence from obtaining licenses. This contributed to a significant increase in public safety, as venues were less likely to employ individuals who posed a risk to patrons or staff. This focus on vetting and background checks wasn't solely about keeping dangerous individuals out of the

industry, but also demonstrated a commitment to the

professionalization of the sector as a whole, reassuring the public that security personnel were held to a higher standard of conduct.

The SIA's influence extended beyond licensing and training. The organization played a crucial role in developing industry best practices, promoting ethical conduct, and disseminating information about security-related issues. This created a greater degree of consistency and professionalism across the industry, leading to improved public perception and trust in security professionals. The organization also worked closely with other agencies, such as law enforcement and local authorities, to improve communication and cooperation in addressing security-related challenges. This collaborative approach fostered a more integrated and effective approach to security management within the wider context of public safety.

The effects of the SIA's influence were not limited solely to the UK. Many other countries have introduced similar

regulatory frameworks for the security industry, reflecting a global trend towards greater standardization and professionalism. While specific regulations vary, the

underlying principles remain consistent: ensuring adequate training, background checks, licensing, and a clear framework for accountability. This international convergence reflects a growing recognition of the importance of a well-regulated security industry in maintaining public safety and order. This international perspective is crucial for understanding the evolution of the industry as a whole. The comparison of various regulatory frameworks highlights the nuances of national contexts and the challenges of achieving consistent standards across different jurisdictions.

However, the implementation of legislation and regulation was not without its challenges. Initial resistance from some parts of the industry, accustomed to a less regulated environment, was common. Concerns were raised about the costs and administrative burdens associated with licensing and training. There were also debates about the adequacy of the training programs and the effectiveness of the regulatory framework in achieving its objectives. These challenges highlighted the ongoing need for adaptation and refinement in the regulatory approach, a process that continues to evolve today. The initial implementation phase involved significant training, education and investment, not only in regulatory bodies, but also in security firms who were required to upgrade their training programs and ensure that their employees met the newly established standards.

In conclusion, the impact of legislation and regulation on the night-time security industry has been transformative. The introduction of formal licensing, mandatory training, and regulatory oversight has professionalized the sector,

improving standards of conduct, enhancing public safety, and reducing the potential for liability. While the journey towards a fully regulated industry has been marked by

challenges and ongoing debates, the overall impact has been overwhelmingly positive, creating a safer and more

responsible environment for both patrons and security

personnel alike. The constant evolution of legislation and regulation reflects the dynamic nature of the night-time economy and the ongoing need for the security industry to adapt and evolve to meet these challenges. The story of the industry's regulatory evolution is far from over, with continuous refinement and adaptation necessary to keep pace with emerging threats and societal changes. The successful integration of technology, ongoing professional development and proactive collaboration with other agencies will ensure

that the industry continues to deliver its vital role in maintaining the safety and vibrancy of the night-time economy.

Camaraderie and Challenges

The transition from a largely unregulated, often haphazard, industry to one governed by stringent licensing and training requirements didn't erase the inherent culture of the night-time security profession. Instead, it shaped and refined it, forging a new kind of camaraderie built on shared professionalism and a collective understanding of the risks involved. This shared experience, born from facing similar challenges and navigating identical legal frameworks, created an unusually strong bond between security personnel. It was a brotherhood, sometimes a sisterhood, forged in the crucible of late nights, unruly crowds, and the ever-present potential for violence.

This unique culture manifested itself in several ways. The shared understanding of the job's inherent dangers fostered a deep sense of mutual respect and reliance. A door supervisor wasn't just a colleague; they were often a potential lifeline in a potentially volatile situation. The unspoken trust, built on countless nights spent navigating the same pressures, was a vital component of the job. A knowing glance, a subtle gesture – these silent communications often spoke volumes in the often-chaotic environment of a busy nightclub or pub.

The informal networks that developed within the industry were crucial to navigating its complexities. Experienced supervisors passed on knowledge and skills, mentoring younger colleagues and sharing their insights into crowd management, conflict resolution, and dealing with intoxicated or aggressive individuals. This informal training, passed down through generations of security professionals, complemented the formal training mandated by the SIA, filling in the gaps and providing a practical, real-world context to the theoretical knowledge imparted in courses. These networks extended beyond individual venues; often, door supervisors from different establishments would exchange information and share experiences, creating a collective wisdom that helped navigate the diverse challenges of the night-time economy.

This sense of shared experience, however, was not without its darker side. The emotional toll of the job was substantial. Security personnel regularly witnessed violence, aggression, and the consequences of excessive alcohol consumption.

They were often the first responders to incidents ranging from minor altercations to serious assaults. This constant exposure to the darker aspects of human behavior took its toll, leading to burnout, stress, and even post-traumatic stress disorder. The stoicism often associated with the profession, a necessity for maintaining composure in high-pressure situations, could also become a barrier to seeking help and support. Many security professionals felt a strong reluctance to discuss their emotional struggles, fearing it might be seen as a weakness or a sign of inadequacy.

The physical demands of the job also contributed to the unique culture. Long hours on their feet, often in

uncomfortable or cramped conditions, were the norm. The physical exertion, coupled with the mental strain of

maintaining vigilance and responding to unexpected

incidents, resulted in a demanding and physically taxing work environment. Many former security personnel

described the job as "wearing," both physically and

emotionally. This physical toll wasn't limited to just fatigue; many experienced back problems, foot injuries, or other ailments arising from the demanding nature of the work. The inherent physical risks were ever-present. A confrontation with a violent individual could lead to serious injury,

requiring the security professional to possess a keen sense of self-preservation coupled with appropriate de-escalation techniques.

The social aspect of the job further contributed to the

distinctive culture. Security personnel were often the unseen guardians of the night-time economy, observing the ebb and flow of human interaction, witnessing both the best and worst of human behavior. While they might not have been the center of attention, their role was vital in ensuring the safety and smooth operation of the venues they protected. The relationships they built with regular patrons and bar staff contributed to a sense of community, a shared understanding of the unspoken rules and rhythms of the night-time world.

These relationships often extended beyond the confines of the workplace, creating a network of support and

camaraderie that extended beyond the official boundaries of the job.

However, this camaraderie wasn't always harmonious.

Internal conflicts and rivalries could arise, sometimes

stemming from competition between different security firms or even individual supervisors vying for recognition or status. Issues of pay and working conditions, a perennial source of tension in many industries, were also prevalent within the security sector. The often-unsociable hours and low pay, coupled with the inherent risks of the job, led to a constant struggle for better working conditions and fairer wages. These struggles often served to unite security

professionals in a common cause, highlighting the

importance of collective action and worker solidarity in addressing industry-wide concerns.

The legal framework surrounding the industry, while

professionalizing the sector, also added another layer of complexity to the cultural landscape. The SIA licensing and training requirements, while designed to improve standards, also introduced a new set of challenges. The constant need to update training, maintain compliance with regulations, and stay abreast of changes in legislation added to the already demanding workload. This emphasis on compliance and accountability created a distinct pressure, forcing security professionals to balance the demands of their job with the stringent requirements of the legal framework. This tension between the practical realities of the job and the demands of the regulatory environment was a constant theme within the security profession, shaping the culture and influencing the professional development of its practitioners.

Furthermore, the increasing use of technology in the security industry also altered the cultural landscape. The introduction of CCTV systems, access control technology, and other electronic surveillance tools changed the way security work was performed. While these advancements improved efficiency and enhanced safety, they also introduced a new set of challenges, requiring security professionals to adapt to new technologies and integrate them into their existing skillset. The reliance on technology didn't negate the importance of human interaction; rather, it created a new blend of human observation and technological monitoring, changing the dynamic of the job and influencing the skills and experience valued within the profession.

The stories of individual security professionals reveal the multifaceted nature of this culture. Accounts from those working in busy city centers differ significantly from those protecting smaller, more rural establishments. The

challenges faced by female security officers, often

navigating a predominantly male environment, presented unique experiences and perspectives. The experiences of older, more established professionals contrasted sharply with the challenges encountered by those entering the profession.

These diverse narratives, gleaned from interviews and

personal accounts, provided a rich tapestry of human

experience, illuminating the complexities of the security profession and adding depth to the understanding of its unique cultural landscape. The common thread throughout these varied experiences remained the shared sense of responsibility, the camaraderie forged in the face of adversity, and the unique bond created through the shared experience of protecting the night-time economy. The industry's evolution, from its unregulated beginnings to a more formalized and regulated profession, only strengthened these bonds, shaping a unique culture built upon shared challenges, mutual respect, and the unwavering commitment to ensuring the safety and well-being of patrons and

colleagues alike.

Early Technological Advancements and Their Impact on Security

The shift towards a more regulated and professional security industry in the latter half of the 20th century wasn't solely driven by changes in legislation and training standards. A parallel evolution occurred in the technological tools available to security personnel, fundamentally altering their working practices and enhancing their effectiveness. This technological advancement, though initially slow and often expensive, proved transformative, marking a gradual transition from a reliance on sheer numbers and physical presence to a more strategic and technologically-assisted approach to security.

One of the earliest and most impactful technological

advancements was the introduction of Closed-Circuit

Television (CCTV). In its early iterations, CCTV was far removed from the sophisticated, high-resolution, networked systems we see today. The initial systems were bulky, grainy, and limited in their range and capabilities. The cameras themselves were often large and conspicuous, more likely to deter casual offenders than provide high-quality evidence for prosecution. The recording equipment was equally cumbersome, requiring significant space and technical expertise to operate and maintain. Despite these limitations, the impact of even these early CCTV systems was significant. For the first time, security personnel had a visual record of events, allowing for improved monitoring of activity and the identification of potential threats or incidents. This shifted the focus from purely reactive responses to a degree of proactive monitoring, allowing supervisors to anticipate problems and intervene before they escalated.

The early adoption of CCTV was largely driven by larger venues, such as nightclubs in major urban areas and larger industrial complexes, where the cost of the technology could be more readily absorbed. Smaller pubs and clubs, particularly those in more rural locations, remained largely reliant on human observation and physical presence for many years. The expense wasn't simply the cost of the equipment itself, but also the associated infrastructure –cabling, power supplies, and dedicated recording spaces. Furthermore, the lack of readily available trained personnel to operate and maintain the systems presented another

significant barrier. The scarcity of trained technicians meant that many early installations struggled with reliability issues, diminishing their overall effectiveness.

However, the advantages were clear, even with the

limitations. The ability to review footage after an incident proved invaluable in investigations, helping to provide

crucial evidence to law enforcement. Furthermore, the mere presence of CCTV cameras often acted as a deterrent, reducing the incidence of crime and disorder. Anecdotal evidence from security professionals of that era suggests that the visual deterrent effect of CCTV was as, if not more, powerful than its evidentiary value in the early years of adoption. Knowing they were being observed, even with relatively low-quality technology, significantly altered the behavior of many potential troublemakers.

Simultaneously, advancements in communication technology dramatically improved the effectiveness of security teams.

The introduction of two-way radios provided a means for instant communication between security personnel across large venues or between multiple security personnel on patrol in a defined area. Prior to this, communication relied on cumbersome methods such as telephone systems or even shouting across distances, making rapid response to

incidents difficult and often unreliable. Two-way radios allowed for immediate coordination and rapid response times, enhancing both security and crowd management. Security teams could rapidly respond to incidents, call for backup, or communicate vital information to each other, creating a more efficient and effective system of crowd control.

The impact of these improved communication systems

extended beyond the immediate response to incidents. It facilitated better coordination of security patrols, allowing for optimized coverage of areas and a more proactive approach to security management. Teams could be deployed strategically to address emerging hotspots or potential trouble areas based on information received through radio communication. This improved coordination allowed for more efficient resource allocation, maximizing the effectiveness of a limited number of security personnel. The ability to maintain constant communication reduced isolation and enhanced the sense of teamwork and camaraderie within security teams. The experience of working together,

communicating effectively, and responding rapidly to

challenges fostered a strong sense of mutual support and reliance.

The evolution of both CCTV and radio communication wasn't a linear progression. Both technologies faced

challenges in terms of affordability, reliability, and the

availability of trained personnel. The initial uptake was gradual, often limited to larger venues with the resources to invest in these new technologies. However, as technology advanced, becoming more reliable, user-friendly, and affordable, its adoption increased exponentially. This gradual integration of technology marked a significant shift in the security industry, enhancing the capabilities of security personnel and improving the overall safety and security of the venues and the people within them. The improved situational awareness afforded by CCTV and the enhanced communication facilitated by two-way radios transformed the night-time security landscape.

Beyond CCTV and radios, other technological

advancements, albeit slower to gain traction, started to

appear on the horizon. These included early access control systems, using keypads or swipe cards, offering a more controlled entry and exit process for designated areas. While still relatively primitive in their design and capabilities compared to today's systems, they represented a move away from the reliance on manual checks and physical barriers. These early systems, while expensive to implement, laid the groundwork for the sophisticated access control systems that are now prevalent in many venues.

The integration of technology into night-time security was not without its challenges. Training staff to operate and maintain the new equipment was crucial. This meant significant investments in training programs and the development of skilled technicians. The industry had to adapt its training programs to include technical aspects alongside the traditional physical and interpersonal skills.

Moreover, issues surrounding data privacy and security began to emerge with the increasing use of CCTV systems. The question of who had access to the footage and how it should be used raised ethical and legal concerns.

Despite these challenges, the early adoption of CCTV, two-way radios, and other technological advancements profoundly altered the nature of night-time security. The shift from a primarily reactive approach, reliant on physical presence and immediate intervention, towards a more

proactive, technologically-assisted strategy fundamentally

changed the work environment and the role of security personnel. It enhanced their capabilities, improving their efficiency and effectiveness in maintaining safety and order.

While the human element remained paramount, the

technological advancements of this era provided the crucial tools that allowed security professionals to better protect patrons and venues alike, shaping the future of the industry in profound ways. The integration of technology wasn't simply about replacing human security personnel; rather, it was about empowering them with the tools needed to operate in a more complex and demanding environment. This marked the beginning of a continuous evolution, a trend that would continue to shape the night-time security industry for decades to come. The fundamental shift towards a technologically-assisted approach marked a watershed moment, transforming the profession and significantly

improving the safety and security of the night-time economy.

The integration of technology became not simply an enhancement but a fundamental component of effective security practice.

Early Training Methods and Their Limitations

The history of security training, particularly for door

supervisors, is a fascinating reflection of the industry's own evolution. Before the formalization of training standards, the learning curve was steep and often haphazard. Early training methods were largely informal, relying heavily on on-the-job experience under the tutelage of more seasoned individuals. This "apprenticeship" model, while effective in some ways, lacked consistency and often perpetuated outdated or even dangerous practices. A young bouncer in a bustling 1970s pub, for instance, might learn more from observing a brawl and its aftermath than from any formal instruction. The emphasis was often on brute strength and intimidation, a far cry from today's emphasis on de-escalation and conflict resolution.

This informal approach had several limitations. Firstly, there was a complete lack of standardization. Training varied dramatically from venue to venue and from supervisor to supervisor, depending on individual experience and the prevailing culture within the establishment. What constituted"effective" crowd control or conflict resolution could vary wildly, resulting in inconsistent practices across the industry.

Some supervisors might emphasize a firm, no-nonsense approach, while others might adopt a more conciliatory style. This lack of uniformity created inconsistencies in security standards and, arguably, increased the risk of incidents.

Secondly, the absence of formalized training often resulted in a skewed and incomplete understanding of legal frameworks and responsibilities. Many early door

supervisors had little to no understanding of the legal aspects of their roles, leading to potential legal issues for both the individual and the venue. Misunderstandings regarding the use of force, arrest powers, and the limitations of authority were commonplace. The consequences could range from minor infractions to serious legal ramifications, including accusations of assault or false imprisonment. This lack of clear legal knowledge exposed both the security personnel and the establishments they protected to potential liability.

Thirdly, the absence of structured training meant there was little emphasis on essential skills beyond physical strength. Crucial skills like communication, conflict de-escalation, and emergency response were largely overlooked. Early training focused primarily on physical capabilities—the ability to handle aggressive individuals, remove disruptive patrons, and maintain order through sheer presence. The critical importance of verbal de-escalation techniques, the effective use of communication to prevent escalation, and the implementation of crowd control strategies were often secondary, if considered at all. This lack of training in non-physical skills contributed to a higher incidence of violent confrontations.

The lack of professional development opportunities

exacerbated these limitations. There were few, if any,

pathways for experienced supervisors to enhance their skills or deepen their knowledge. Continuous learning and professional growth were not widely acknowledged as important. This resulted in a stagnant workforce, where skills remained largely static, failing to adapt to the changing dynamics of the nightlife economy. The challenges of the job were often met with the same reactive solutions, regardless of evolving social norms or societal changes. A reliance on traditional methods, lacking both nuance and adaptability, meant that potential for conflict remained consistently high.

The rise of professional security firms in the late 20th century signaled a gradual shift toward more formalized training. These firms, recognizing the need for consistent standards and improved practices, began to implement rudimentary training programs for their employees. These programs were a far cry from the rigorous standards of today, but they represented a crucial step towards professionalism. They often incorporated elements of basic conflict resolution, communication skills, and rudimentary legal knowledge. However, the quality and scope of these programs varied considerably, and the industry as a whole lacked a unifying, overarching framework for training and certification.

The introduction of the Security Industry Authority (SIA) in the UK in 2001 marked a watershed moment. The SIA's establishment brought about significant changes, not only through the introduction of mandatory licensing but also through the standardization of training courses and qualifications. The SIA licensing scheme ensured that

individuals working in the security industry met minimum competency standards, receiving formal training in areas such as conflict management, crowd control, legal powers, and health and safety. The focus shifted dramatically from brute force to a more nuanced, skills-based approach.

Comparing early training practices with modern SIA-

approved courses highlights the dramatic transformation in the security industry. The rudimentary, often ad-hoc training of the past has given way to structured, competency-based learning. Modern courses utilize a mix of classroom instruction, practical exercises, and role-playing scenarios to equip security personnel with the skills necessary to handle various challenges. The curriculum covers a vast range of topics, including:

Legal Powers and Responsibilities:

A thorough understanding of the legal framework governing security operations, including the powers of arrest, use of force, and data protection regulations.

Conflict Management and De-escalation:

Techniques for preventing and de-escalating conflicts, including verbal de-escalation, communication strategies, and non-violent intervention methods.

Crowd Management and Control:

Strategies for managing large crowds, ensuring safety, and preventing incidents such as crushing or panic.

Health and Safety:

Awareness of health and safety regulations, risk assessment procedures, and emergency response protocols.

Customer Service and Communication:

Emphasis on professional conduct, effective communication with patrons, and conflict resolution techniques.

First Aid and Emergency Response:

The ability to administer basic first aid and to respond effectively to various emergencies, including medical emergencies, fire, and violence.

Physical Intervention Techniques (controlled and

proportionate):

While physical intervention remains a necessary component of security work, modern training emphasizes the use of proportionate and controlled physical techniques only as a last resort.

Terrorism Awareness:

Training now includes modules addressing the recognition and response to potential terrorist threats and security incidents.

The emphasis on professionalism and accountability has profoundly impacted the industry. The SIA's licensing and training standards have elevated the reputation of door supervisors, reducing instances of unprofessional behavior and promoting a more responsible approach to security. It also fostered a sense of professional pride and identity amongst those working in the sector, leading to improved recruitment and retention rates. The SIA's ongoing oversight and monitoring continue to maintain and strengthen these standards, constantly adapting to the evolving demands of the night-time economy. The journey from rudimentary on-the-job training to the sophisticated, regulated training environment of today represents a significant milestone in the history of security within the nightlife industry, marking a transition from an era of physical dominance to one of informed, skills-based practice. The limitations of the past serve as a reminder of the importance of rigorous training and consistent standards in ensuring a safe and professional security environment.

The Role of the SIA in Shaping Professional Standards

The establishment of the Security Industry Authority (SIA) in 2001 marked a watershed moment in the history of the UK security industry. Prior to its creation, the sector operated with a patchwork of regulations and varying levels of training, leading to inconsistencies in professional standards and a lack of accountability. The SIA's mandate was clear: to regulate the private security industry, ensuring that individuals working in licensed security roles possessed the necessary skills, knowledge, and ethical understanding to perform their duties effectively and responsibly. This involved establishing a licensing system, setting minimum training standards, and developing a robust enforcement mechanism to address breaches of regulations.

The impact of the SIA was immediate and transformative.

The introduction of compulsory licensing for specific

security roles, including door supervisors, immediately raised the bar for entry into the profession. No longer could individuals simply assume the role of a bouncer with minimal or no training; they were now required to undergo a vetting process, including criminal record checks, and complete a recognised training course covering areas such as conflict management, communication skills, legal powers, and health and safety. This comprehensive training program, designed and approved by the SIA, aimed to replace the ad-hoc, often inadequate, methods of the past.

The SIA's impact extended beyond just initial training. The licensing scheme also introduced a system of ongoing professional development. Licensees were required to maintain their professional competence through continuous learning and updated knowledge, ensuring their skills

remained relevant and effective in addressing evolving

security challenges. This ongoing professional development has played a key role in adapting to new technology, legislation, and best practices within the security sector. The requirement to maintain a license incentivized security professionals to remain updated in their knowledge and skills, leading to higher levels of professional conduct within the industry.

One significant area where the SIA's influence is clearly visible is in the reduction of violence and disorder in

licensed premises. The emphasis on de-escalation

techniques, conflict resolution strategies, and communication skills during training has significantly reduced incidents of aggression and violence linked to security personnel. Prior to the introduction of the SIA, the industry often relied on brute force and intimidation as primary methods of conflict resolution. This approach, while sometimes effective in the short-term, often exacerbated problems and led to further violence. The SIA's training standards shifted the paradigm, promoting a more preventative and proactive approach to security, focusing on identifying potential conflicts before they escalated. The emphasis on verbal communication skills, coupled with an understanding of relevant legislation and the appropriate use of force, has significantly altered the way door supervisors engage with patrons.

The enforcement arm of the SIA has also played a crucial role in upholding professional standards. The Authority possesses powers to investigate complaints against licensed individuals, revoke licenses for breaches of regulations, and take action against companies operating without the necessary permits. This system of accountability has drastically reduced the instances of rogue operators and individuals engaging in unprofessional or illegal activities.

The SIA's ability to sanction individuals and businesses serves as a deterrent, fostering a culture of compliance and responsibility within the industry. The potential loss of a license, representing a significant loss of livelihood, ensures that licensees are incentivized to uphold the high standards set by the SIA. Regular audits and inspections by the SIA further reinforce these standards, ensuring that training providers maintain high levels of quality and that security companies adhere to the licensing requirements.

However, the SIA's influence hasn't been without its challenges. The initial implementation of the licensing scheme encountered resistance from some sectors of the industry, particularly those accustomed to the less regulated environment of the past. Concerns were raised about the cost and time involved in obtaining a license, leading to some individuals leaving the industry. However, the long-term benefits of improved professional standards and enhanced public safety have clearly outweighed the initial challenges.

Furthermore, the SIA continually adapts to the changing landscape of the security industry. The rapid advancements in technology, such as the increasing use of CCTV and other electronic security systems, have required the SIA to update its training standards accordingly. The integration of new technologies into training programs ensures that security personnel possess the skills and knowledge to effectively utilize these tools in a safe and responsible manner. The SIA also remains vigilant in addressing emerging threats and challenges within the industry. The rise of new forms of crime and disorder, such as online harassment and cyber security threats, has led the SIA to incorporate these topics into training, reflecting the evolving nature of the security profession.

Another notable impact of the SIA is the professionalization of the industry as a whole. Prior to the implementation of the licensing scheme, the security industry was often viewed with suspicion and even disdain. The lack of formal training and regulation fostered a perception of the sector as poorly trained and unprofessional. The SIA's work has significantly challenged this perception. By setting high standards of training, promoting ethical conduct, and enforcing

compliance, the SIA has helped to elevate the status of

security professionals. This is further evidenced by improved recruitment practices within the security industry, as individuals are now more likely to consider a career path within the regulated sector, particularly given the enhanced training and career opportunities offered.

The SIA's impact is not simply measured in terms of reduced violence and improved training but also in the contribution it has made to the broader economy. The improved professionalism of the sector has attracted higher-quality individuals, leading to increased productivity and effectiveness. Moreover, the regulatory framework has ensured a level playing field for businesses, fostering fair competition and discouraging unscrupulous practices. This in turn enhances consumer confidence and contributes to the overall stability and prosperity of the night-time economy. The increased safety and security provided by professionally trained and licensed personnel ensures that venues are more attractive to customers, thereby bolstering businesses reliant on the night-time economy.

The SIA's work in shaping the professionalism of door supervisors and other security professionals extends beyond the immediate impact of licensing and training. The establishment of a robust complaints procedure has provided a mechanism for addressing grievances and ensuring accountability. This process allows individuals to voice concerns about unprofessional conduct or alleged

misconduct by security personnel, providing a system of checks and balances that promotes ethical practice within the sector. The SIA's investigation into such complaints fosters a culture of responsibility and encourages security professionals to adhere to high ethical standards. The transparency of the SIA's processes, coupled with the ability to pursue formal complaints, provides an assurance of accountability for both licensees and the security companies employing them.

In conclusion, the SIA's role in shaping professional

standards within the security industry has been nothing short of transformative. By establishing a robust licensing and training framework, enforcing regulations, and promoting ethical conduct, the SIA has not only improved the safety and security of the night-time economy but also significantly elevated the professional standing of security personnel. The transition from an industry characterized by informal practices and inconsistent standards to one underpinned by rigorous training and accountability marks a significant achievement, showcasing the powerful role of regulation in promoting professionalism and ensuring public safety. The continuous adaptation of the SIA's standards to address evolving threats and technological advancements ensures that the security industry remains relevant and effective in safeguarding the public. The legacy of the SIA is one of increased safety, improved professionalism, and a more responsible and accountable security industry. The long-term consequences of its establishment are evident in the safer, more regulated, and ultimately, more professional night-time economy of today.

The Development of Specialized Security Training

The SIA's establishment dramatically altered the landscape of security training, moving away from the ad-hoc, often inconsistent approaches of the past. Before 2001, training varied wildly depending on the employer, ranging from minimal on-the-job instruction to more comprehensive programs offered by private training providers, the quality of which could be highly variable. Consistency was largely absent, leading to significant discrepancies in the skills and knowledge possessed by security personnel across different venues and regions. This lack of standardization posed a risk to public safety and hindered the development of a truly professional security industry.

The SIA's introduction of mandatory licensing and

standardized training curricula addressed these shortcomings directly. The licensing system ensured that all security personnel working in licensed roles met minimum competency requirements, while the standardized training provided a common foundation of knowledge and skills. This marked a significant step towards professionalism and accountability within the sector. The new training programs moved beyond basic security procedures and incorporated modules on legal frameworks, conflict resolution, communication skills, and ethical conduct. This broader scope reflected a growing recognition that effective security personnel needed to be more than just enforcers; they needed to be skilled communicators, conflict mediators, and

responsible members of the community.

The initial training standards, however, were relatively basic and lacked the specialization required for the diverse settings within the night-time economy. While the foundation provided by the SIA was essential, the need for more

specialized training quickly became apparent. Nightclubs, for instance, presented a unique set of challenges,

demanding expertise in crowd management, dealing with intoxication, and managing volatile situations. Pubs, on the other hand, often faced different issues, including dealing with minor disturbances, preventing underage drinking, and ensuring the safety of patrons in a potentially less controlled environment. Large-scale events, such as concerts and festivals, presented an even greater scale of challenges, requiring specialized training in crowd control, emergency response, and coordinating with emergency services.

This led to the development of specialized training programs tailored to the specific needs of different venues and event types. Private training providers began offering more specialized courses, focusing on areas such as conflict de-escalation, advanced crowd management techniques, and the use of CCTV and other security technologies. These courses built upon the core competencies established by the SIA but provided the additional skills and knowledge necessary for dealing with the unique challenges presented by particular environments.

The increasing sophistication of security threats also played a significant role in shaping specialized training programs. The rise of terrorism, for example, led to a greater emphasis on counter-terrorism awareness training. Security personnel were trained to recognize potential threats, report suspicious activity, and respond effectively in emergency situations. The growing use of technology in security operations also necessitated the development of specialized training programs focused on the use of CCTV systems, access control systems, and other security technologies. This ensured that security personnel were proficient in using the latest technologies to enhance security effectiveness.

The training landscape continued to evolve as technology advanced and new challenges emerged. The rise of social media and its impact on conflict escalation and reputation management required training to address these modern phenomena. Training now incorporates the effective use of social media in incident reporting and crisis communication, alongside strategies for mitigating the spread of misinformation or negative publicity. The use of body-worn cameras also necessitated training on their proper operation, legal implications, and ethical considerations. Furthermore, advancements in security technology, such as facial recognition systems and predictive policing tools, have led to the need for specialized training in their effective and ethical deployment.

Specialized training also extends beyond the purely technical aspects of security work. Increasingly, there is a recognition of the importance of emotional intelligence and interpersonal skills in effective security practice. Training now incorporates modules on communication skills, empathy, and conflict resolution, recognizing the critical role these skills play in de-escalating potentially violent situations and maintaining positive relationships with patrons and colleagues. Furthermore, the emphasis on diversity and inclusion has led to training programs that promote awareness of unconscious bias and cultural sensitivity, ensuring that security personnel can interact effectively with diverse populations.

The growth of corporate security has also spurred the

development of specialized training programs tailored to the corporate environment. Corporate security settings

frequently require a different skill set compared to the night-time economy, emphasizing access control, asset protection, and the investigation of internal theft or fraud. Training in corporate security often involves modules on risk

assessment, security audits, and emergency response

planning within a corporate context. Additionally,

maintaining confidentiality and adhering to strict corporate protocols are crucial components of corporate security training.

The evolution of specialized security training is a continuous process, driven by the ever-changing needs of the security industry and the evolving nature of threats. Training providers are constantly updating their curricula to reflect the latest best practices, technological advancements, and legal requirements. This necessitates ongoing professional development for security personnel, ensuring they maintain their skills and knowledge. Regular refresher courses and advanced training opportunities are crucial in maintaining the highest standards of professionalism and competence.

The impact of specialized training is evident in the improved professionalism and effectiveness of the security industry.

The higher standards have increased public confidence in security personnel and enhanced the safety and security of the venues and events they protect. The move toward a more professionalized industry has been instrumental in improving the image and status of security personnel. It has enabled them to move beyond the stereotypical view of the bouncer or security guard, fostering recognition for the crucial role they play in maintaining public order and safety.

The continuous adaptation of specialized security training has been vital in addressing the challenges of a complex and dynamic environment. From the rudimentary methods of the past to the sophisticated training programs of today, the security industry has undergone a significant transformation. This evolution reflects a greater understanding of the diverse roles and responsibilities of security personnel, along with an increased appreciation of the value of highly skilled and well-trained professionals. The ongoing development of specialized training is a testament to the commitment to enhancing public safety and maintaining a professional and accountable security industry. The emphasis on continuous learning and professional development ensures that the industry remains at the forefront of innovation and is well-equipped to tackle the ever-evolving challenges of the 21st century. The future of security training will undoubtedly involve even greater specialization, adapting to new technologies and threats, and placing an even stronger emphasis on ethical considerations and responsible practice.

The pursuit of excellence in security training remains a continuous journey, reflecting the ongoing commitment to protecting communities and ensuring a safer environment for all.

The development of specialized security training programs has also involved close collaboration between training providers, the SIA, and the security industry itself. Feedback from security professionals working in different settings has been instrumental in shaping the content and structure of training courses, ensuring that they remain relevant and effective. This collaborative approach has facilitated a constant refinement of training standards, reflecting the dynamic and evolving needs of the security industry. Regular reviews and updates to the training curricula guarantee that security personnel receive the most up-to-date knowledge and skills to effectively and ethically perform their duties.

Furthermore, the increasing recognition of the importance of mental health within the security industry has led to the integration of well-being and resilience training into many programs. The demanding and often stressful nature of security work can take a toll on mental health, so training now often includes modules on stress management, coping mechanisms, and access to support services. This holistic approach to training acknowledges the importance of supporting the well-being of security personnel, thereby enhancing their effectiveness and job satisfaction. The inclusion of such components highlights a broader shift toward prioritizing the mental health of security professionals, reflecting a more compassionate and supportive approach within the industry.

The evolution of specialized security training is a continuing process, shaped by technological advancements, shifting societal needs, and a growing understanding of the complexities inherent in security work. The journey from rudimentary on-the-job training to highly specialized, comprehensive programs reflects not just an improvement in technical skills, but also a broader shift toward a more ethical, professional, and supportive approach within the security industry. The development of specialized training programs is a crucial element in shaping a safer and more secure society.

Continuing Professional Development CPD in Security

The establishment of the Security Industry Authority (SIA) in 2001 marked a watershed moment, not just in terms of initial training and licensing, but also in the ongoing professional development of security personnel. Prior to this, the concept of continuing professional development (CPD) was largely absent from the security landscape. While some forward-thinking companies might have offered in-house refresher courses or encouraged staff to attend relevant industry events, these were far from standardized or mandatory. The lack of a structured approach to CPD reflected a broader lack of professionalization within the sector. Security work was often viewed as a stepping-stone, a temporary job rather than a career, and this perception was reflected in the limited investment in ongoing training and development.

The SIA's licensing regime, however, fundamentally

changed this equation. By requiring individuals to hold valid SIA licenses to work in the security industry, the authority implicitly acknowledged the need for ongoing competence.

The license itself wasn't a lifetime guarantee; it required periodic renewal, and this renewal process was directly linked to the completion of relevant CPD activities. This move forced a paradigm shift, transforming the security profession from a largely unregulated, informally trained field to one demanding consistent updating of knowledge and skills. This was a significant step towards

professionalization, boosting the overall credibility and standing of security personnel.

The requirement for CPD, however, extended beyond mere license renewal. It emphasized the dynamic nature of the security profession. The threat landscape is constantly evolving, new technologies are constantly emerging, and legislative changes frequently necessitate updates to procedures and practices. From advancements in CCTV technology and access control systems to changes in legislation regarding public order and terrorism prevention, security professionals must adapt to remain effective and competent. Failing to engage in CPD meant falling behind, risking incompetence, and potentially jeopardizing public safety.

The types of CPD available to security personnel have

become increasingly diverse and sophisticated. Traditional methods, such as attending conferences and workshops, remain popular. These events often bring together leading experts in the field, offering valuable insights into the latest trends, techniques, and challenges. They also provide opportunities for networking and sharing best practices amongst security professionals, fostering a sense of community and shared professional identity—a vital element in what was previously a relatively isolated and fragmented workforce. The collaborative element, born out of shared experiences and professional development, strengthens not only individual competence but also industry standards.

Beyond conferences and workshops, online learning

platforms have emerged as a significant resource for CPD.

These platforms offer a flexible and accessible way for security personnel to enhance their skills and knowledge at their own pace and convenience. The availability of online modules covering a wide range of topics, from conflict management and communication skills to advanced surveillance techniques and cyber security, caters to the varied needs of security professionals at different levels of experience. The ability to access these resources remotely, often at minimal cost, has democratized access to professional development and broken down barriers that previously limited opportunities for training.

The development of specialized CPD programs tailored to specific roles and responsibilities within the security sector has also been a notable advancement. For example, door supervisors can access specialized training in conflict resolution, crowd management, and the legal aspects of their role. CCTV operators can receive enhanced training in image analysis, surveillance techniques, and data protection.

Similarly, those working in close protection or corporate security can receive specialized training in risk assessment, personal security, and advanced security technologies. This specialized training allows security personnel to hone their expertise in specific areas, enhancing their effectiveness and contributing to a more efficient and capable security

workforce.

Furthermore, the increasing integration of technology in security operations has made CPD in this area essential.

Security systems are becoming increasingly sophisticated, utilizing advanced technologies like AI-powered surveillance systems, biometric access control, and predictive analytics. Security professionals must be equipped to understand, operate, and maintain these technologies effectively, requiring continuous updating of their knowledge base. This isn't limited to the technical aspects; the ethical implications of using such technology, including data privacy and potential bias in algorithms, must also be considered as part of ongoing training.

The emphasis on CPD within the security industry is also reflected in the growing number of professional bodies and accreditations. These organizations play a crucial role in setting standards, providing professional guidance, and promoting best practices within the sector. Membership in these bodies often necessitates ongoing CPD, further

reinforcing the importance of continuous learning and professional development. These certifications, in turn, become valuable credentials, helping security professionals to stand out in a competitive job market and potentially command higher salaries reflecting their expertise and commitment to professional excellence.

However, the provision of CPD is not without its challenges. Access to training, particularly for those working in smaller or less financially secure companies, can be an issue. The cost of courses and the time required to attend training can pose obstacles for individuals who may already work long and irregular hours. The industry itself, with its characteristically high employee turnover, also presents challenges in ensuring consistent participation in CPD programs.

Addressing these challenges necessitates a multi-pronged approach. Collaboration between the SIA, training providers, and employers is crucial. Employers must prioritize and actively support CPD for their staff, providing both the financial resources and the necessary time off for training. The SIA could explore initiatives to subsidize training costs for individuals or smaller companies, potentially through grants or loan schemes. Greater flexibility in the delivery of CPD, including online modules and blended learning approaches, is also vital in making training more accessible and accommodating to the diverse needs and schedules of security professionals.

In conclusion, continuing professional development is no longer a luxury but a necessity within the security industry. The evolving threat landscape, advancements in technology, and the growing emphasis on professionalism necessitate a commitment to ongoing training and development. The SIA's role in mandating CPD has been instrumental in

driving this change, but further collaboration and innovation are needed to ensure that all security professionals have access to the high-quality CPD they need to maintain their competence, enhance their skills, and contribute to a safer and more secure society. The transformation of the security sector from a loosely regulated collection of individuals into a profession that values consistent training and continuous improvement is a testament to the hard work and dedication of many. The commitment to CPD represents not just a raising of industry standards, but a commitment to

professionalism and public safety. The ongoing refinement of CPD programs will continue to shape the future of security, reflecting the evolving needs of a dynamic and increasingly complex world.

Emerging Technologies and Challenges

The landscape of security training is poised for a dramatic shift, driven by technological advancements and evolving societal needs. The relatively recent emphasis on continuing professional development (CPD), while a significant step forward, only scratches the surface of what's required to equip security personnel for the challenges ahead. The future of security training demands a proactive, adaptable approach, one that anticipates and integrates emerging technologies and anticipates evolving threat landscapes.

One of the most significant areas of change lies in the

integration of technology. Artificial intelligence (AI) is rapidly transforming security operations, offering tools for predictive policing, facial recognition, and advanced

surveillance systems. Training programs must incorporate modules specifically designed to equip security personnel with the knowledge and skills needed to effectively utilize these technologies. This isn't simply a matter of learning how to operate a piece of software; it requires a deeper understanding of AI's capabilities and limitations, ethical implications, and potential biases. For instance, security personnel need to be trained to identify potential inaccuracies or misinterpretations of AI-driven threat assessments, understanding that these systems are tools, not infallible oracles. Similarly, the ethical considerations surrounding the use of facial recognition technology, data privacy concerns, and the potential for algorithmic bias must be thoroughly addressed in training programs.

Beyond AI, the increasing reliance on CCTV systems, drone surveillance, and other sophisticated monitoring

technologies presents another crucial area for training.

Security personnel will need comprehensive training on the operation, maintenance, and legal implications of these systems. This includes understanding data protection regulations, protocols for handling sensitive information, and the responsible use of surveillance technology to avoid infringement on individual rights. The effectiveness of these technologies relies heavily on the training received by the personnel using them; a poorly trained operator can render even the most sophisticated system useless, or worse, lead to misinterpretations that have legal and ethical repercussions.

Furthermore, the growing prevalence of cyber threats

presents a new and significant challenge to the security industry. Security personnel, especially those working in high-security environments, need training on cybersecurity threats, including phishing scams, malware attacks, and data breaches. Understanding the vulnerabilities of digital systems and implementing appropriate security protocols is crucial to prevent incidents. This extends beyond simply recognizing phishing emails; it encompasses a broader understanding of network security, data encryption, and incident response protocols. Training programs must

incorporate realistic scenarios and simulations to prepare security personnel for the complexities of dealing with cyberattacks.

The training must also adapt to the evolving nature of crime. Traditional approaches to security training often focused on reactive measures—responding to incidents as they occur.

However, the future demands a more proactive approach, encompassing preventative strategies and risk assessment.

Security personnel need to be trained in risk assessment methodologies, understanding the factors that contribute to crime in specific environments and developing strategies to mitigate those risks. This might involve training in conflict resolution, de-escalation techniques, and community engagement strategies. The shift toward proactive crime prevention aligns with the increasing emphasis on community policing and the need for security professionals to collaborate effectively with law enforcement and other community stakeholders.

Beyond technological advancements and evolving crime patterns, the future of security training must also address the increasing demand for professionalism and ethical conduct.

The security industry has historically faced challenges in terms of professionalism, and robust training programs can play a pivotal role in improving the industry's image and building public trust. This requires integrating modules on ethical decision-making, cultural sensitivity, and effective communication skills. Security personnel need to understand the legal and ethical boundaries of their roles, ensuring that their actions align with the law and uphold human rights. They must be equipped to deal with diverse populations and handle situations with empathy and professionalism,

particularly those involving vulnerable individuals.

Moreover, training should emphasize the importance of accurate record-keeping and reporting procedures, ensuring that incidents are documented thoroughly and accurately. This is crucial for maintaining accountability and providing valuable data for future crime prevention initiatives.

The challenges in delivering effective future-oriented

security training are considerable. One major hurdle is the cost of training. Advanced technology training, cybersecurity modules, and specialized courses can be expensive, particularly for smaller security firms with

limited budgets. Finding qualified instructors with expertise in emerging technologies and crime trends is also a considerable challenge. Furthermore, the rapid pace of technological change necessitates continuous updates and revisions to training programs, which adds to the ongoing cost and requires a constant commitment to professional development for instructors themselves. Finding the right balance between theoretical knowledge and practical skills is another challenge. While understanding the theoretical underpinnings of AI or cybersecurity is important, it's equally important to ensure that security personnel have sufficient hands-on experience and practical training.

Overcoming these challenges requires a collaborative

approach. Government bodies, industry associations,

educational institutions, and technology providers must work together to develop and deliver high-quality, affordable training programs. Government funding and incentives could be crucial in supporting the development of training programs and ensuring that security personnel have access to the latest technologies and training resources. Industry associations can play a pivotal role in establishing industry-wide standards and best practices, ensuring that training programs are consistent and meet the needs of the industry as a whole. Educational institutions can develop specialized training programs and curricula, incorporating emerging technologies and evolving crime trends into their courses.

Technology providers can offer training and support to security personnel, ensuring that they are proficient in using the latest security technologies.

Furthermore, the industry needs to address the issue of attracting and retaining talent. The security industry has, for a long time, struggled with a perception of being low-skilled and low-paid, leading to high turnover rates. Improving training standards and career progression opportunities can help to attract and retain skilled professionals. This involves creating clear career pathways, providing opportunities for advancement, and rewarding high-performing individuals. It also requires a cultural shift within the industry, promoting a culture of professionalism and recognizing the value of security personnel's contributions. The ongoing professional development opportunities that result from continuous training can be a significant factor in improving employee morale and reducing turnover.

In conclusion, the future of security training is dynamic and multifaceted, demanding a proactive and adaptable

approach. Integrating emerging technologies, anticipating evolving crime trends, and fostering a culture of professionalism are crucial to equip security personnel for the challenges and opportunities of the future. Addressing the financial, logistical, and pedagogical challenges through collaboration will be vital in ensuring that the security industry continues to adapt and maintain a high standard of professionalism and public safety. The success of these efforts will depend not only on the quality of training

programs but also on the ongoing commitment of

individuals, organizations, and governments to invest in a skilled and ethical security workforce. Only then can we guarantee the safe and secure environment vital for our thriving nightlife and public spaces.

The Integration of CCTV and Surveillance Systems

The integration of Closed-Circuit Television (CCTV) and other surveillance systems has fundamentally reshaped the security landscape, particularly within the vibrant and often-challenging environment of the night-time economy. From its humble beginnings as a rudimentary technological advancement, CCTV has evolved into a sophisticated and multifaceted tool, significantly impacting how security professionals operate and how venues manage risk. This evolution hasn't been without its complexities, however, raising significant ethical considerations alongside its

practical benefits.

Early implementations of CCTV were often limited in scope and technological capability. Think grainy black-and-white images, limited viewing angles, and cumbersome recording systems that required significant manual intervention. These early systems were primarily deployed as a reactive measure, used more for post-incident investigation than proactive crime prevention. For example, a pub owner might install a single camera overlooking the bar area to review footage in the event of a robbery. The focus was on evidence gathering, rather than real-time monitoring and preventative security.

This was further hampered by the lack of readily available digital storage and the limitations in transmitting footage across distances. The recording process itself was often manual, requiring the physical rewinding and reviewing of tapes, a process that was both time-consuming and laborious.

The shift towards digital technology marked a significant turning point. The introduction of digital video recorders (DVRs) and Network Video Recorders (NVRs) dramatically improved image quality, storage capacity, and remote

viewing capabilities. This allowed security personnel to monitor multiple cameras simultaneously, from a central location, significantly enhancing their situational awareness.

The development of higher-resolution cameras, improved lighting technology, and sophisticated analytics software further boosted the effectiveness of CCTV systems. Venues could now employ a far more comprehensive approach to security, transitioning from reactive to proactive crime prevention.

The advancement of analytics capabilities has been

particularly transformative. Modern CCTV systems are no longer simply recording visual data; they are actively analyzing it in real time. This includes features such as motion detection, facial recognition, and object tracking.

These analytical tools allow security personnel to receive immediate alerts about suspicious activity, enabling them to respond swiftly and effectively. For instance, a system might trigger an alert if it detects an individual loitering near an exit for an extended period, or if it identifies a known troublemaker entering the premises. This level of proactive monitoring is a far cry from the early days of CCTV, when security relied heavily on observation alone.

However, this increased sophistication has brought a range of ethical considerations to the forefront. The use of facial recognition technology, in particular, raises significant privacy concerns. The potential for misidentification, the possibility of biased algorithms, and the lack of transparency surrounding data usage are all critical issues that require careful consideration and robust legal frameworks. Similarly, the potential for constant surveillance to have a chilling effect on freedom of expression and assembly is an important aspect that needs to be addressed. The implementation of CCTV systems must be balanced against the fundamental rights of individuals, and this balance requires ongoing discussion and legal refinement.

The legal framework surrounding CCTV and surveillance is constantly evolving, reflecting the technological

advancements and ethical challenges. Data Protection Acts and other legislation aim to balance the need for security with the protection of individual privacy. These regulations often dictate how CCTV footage can be collected, stored, accessed, and used. Compliance with these regulations is paramount for both venues and security companies. This requires comprehensive training for staff, the implementation of clear data protection policies, and regular audits to ensure compliance. Furthermore, the clarity of signage informing patrons of CCTV surveillance is crucial to maintaining transparency and managing public expectations.

The practical application of CCTV in the night-time

economy varies widely depending on the type of venue and the specific security challenges faced. Nightclubs, with their large crowds and potential for disorder, may employ extensive CCTV coverage, both inside and outside the premises. Pubs and bars might utilize a more targeted

approach, focusing on areas such as the bar itself, entrances, and exits. Larger events, such as concerts or festivals, often require sophisticated CCTV systems integrated with crowd management strategies and emergency response protocols.

The specific configuration of the system, the number of cameras, and the location of cameras are tailored to address the unique security requirements of each venue.

The use of CCTV is not confined to simply capturing video footage. Integration with other security systems, such as access control systems and alarm systems, allows for a more comprehensive and coordinated approach. For instance, an access control system might trigger an alert if an unauthorized individual attempts to enter a restricted area, and this alert can be immediately relayed to security personnel monitoring the CCTV footage. This integrated approach provides a more holistic picture of the security situation, enabling a more efficient and proactive response.

Beyond the technical capabilities of the systems, the

effectiveness of CCTV relies heavily on the competence and training of security personnel. Security guards need to be trained in how to effectively monitor CCTV feeds, interpret the footage, and respond appropriately to any incidents observed. This includes understanding the limitations of the technology, as well as its potential to provide valuable evidence in case of an incident. Effective training should incorporate knowledge of data protection regulations, ethical considerations, and the best practices for operating and maintaining the systems.

In summary, the integration of CCTV and other surveillance systems has significantly enhanced the security capabilities within the night-time economy. However, this advancement is not without its complexities. Navigating the ethical considerations, understanding the legal framework, and implementing the technology effectively requires a careful and nuanced approach. The ongoing evolution of the technology, combined with the need for adequate training and ethical awareness, underscores the dynamic and multifaceted nature of security in the modern world. The focus must remain on balancing the significant benefits of enhanced security with the fundamental rights and freedoms of the public, a delicate balance that requires continuous vigilance and adaptation.

Access Control Systems and Their Evolution

The evolution of access control systems mirrors the broader technological advancements shaping the security landscape of the night-time economy. Initially, rudimentary methods dominated – simple locks, bouncers relying on memory and observation, and perhaps a handwritten guest list. These systems, while effective to a degree, were inherently limited in their capacity to manage large crowds, accurately identify individuals, and maintain detailed records. The potential for human error, bias, and even collusion was significant,

creating vulnerabilities that sophisticated access control systems were designed to address.

The introduction of key card systems marked a turning point.

These systems, initially prevalent in corporate settings, gradually found their way into nightclubs, bars, and other venues within the night-time economy. The ability to issue and revoke access electronically offered a significant improvement over traditional method. Key cards offered a more streamlined entry process, reducing bottlenecks and improving efficiency. Moreover, they provided a detailed audit trail, allowing venue managers to track who entered and exited the premises, valuable information in the event of incidents or investigations. The transition wasn't without its challenges. The early key card systems were prone to malfunctions, often requiring substantial investment in infrastructure and ongoing maintenance. Concerns about card duplication and unauthorized access also needed to be addressed. However, the benefits gradually outweighed the limitations, and key card systems rapidly gained popularity.

The next major leap forward came with the integration of biometric technology. Biometric scanners, utilizing fingerprint, iris, or facial recognition, offered a higher level of security than traditional key card systems. These systems eliminated the risks associated with lost or stolen cards and significantly reduced the potential for unauthorized entry.

The ability to accurately and instantaneously verify an

individual's identity proved invaluable, especially in

environments where security concerns were paramount. However, the adoption of biometric technology also raised ethical and privacy concerns. The collection and storage of sensitive biometric data required robust security protocols to prevent unauthorized access and misuse. The potential for bias in these systems, and the impact on individuals whose biometric data might not be easily read by the scanner also became significant factors. These concerns led to stringent regulations and guidelines surrounding the implementation of biometric access control systems, emphasizing data

security, transparency, and accountability.

The increasing sophistication of access control systems also brought about the development of integrated security management systems. These systems combine various security technologies, including access control, CCTV, alarm systems, and intruder detection, into a single unified platform. This integration allows for centralized monitoring and control, improving situational awareness and response times. Data from different systems can be correlated to provide a more comprehensive understanding of events, facilitating more effective investigations and risk management. For example, if an unauthorized entry is detected by the access control system, the integrated system can automatically trigger the recording of CCTV footage from relevant cameras, providing valuable evidence for investigations.

The digitalization of access control systems has also led to significant advancements in remote management capabilities. Venue managers can now monitor and control access from remote locations, allowing for greater flexibility and responsiveness. This is particularly beneficial in situations where multiple venues are managed by a single security team, allowing for efficient resource allocation and coordination. Moreover, remote management capabilities enable proactive security measures such as scheduling access permissions based on time, day, or other relevant criteria, enhancing overall security and reducing the workload on security personnel.

Beyond the technological advancements, the evolution of access control systems also reflects a shift in security

philosophy. The focus has moved from solely preventing unauthorized entry to creating a more holistic security

strategy that encompasses various aspects of risk

management. Access control is no longer viewed in

isolation, but as an integrated component of a larger security system designed to protect people, assets, and operations. The night-time economy, with its inherent complexities and risks, demands a multifaceted approach that goes beyond the simple act of controlling access.

Furthermore, the integration of access control systems with other technologies, like mobile applications and social media platforms, is transforming how venues manage access and engage with their patrons. Mobile ticketing and digital registration systems are increasingly common, offering convenience and efficiency for patrons while simultaneously enhancing security through verifiable digital credentials. This trend reflects a growing reliance on digital technologies to manage the complexities of the night-time economy, streamlining operations and improving security protocols.

However, this digitalization also brings new challenges relating to cybersecurity, data protection, and the potential for digital manipulation or fraud, requiring constant

vigilance and adaptation to keep ahead of evolving threats.

The ongoing evolution of access control systems is driven by factors such as increasing security threats, technological advancements, and evolving regulatory requirements. The development of artificial intelligence (AI) and machine learning (ML) is poised to significantly impact the future of access control. AI-powered systems can analyze vast amounts of data to identify patterns and anomalies, enabling predictive policing and proactive security measures. For example, an AI-powered system could analyze access patterns to identify potential security breaches or predict areas of heightened risk, enabling proactive interventions by security personnel. However, the deployment of AI and ML in access control raises new ethical considerations, particularly regarding bias, transparency, and accountability. The potential for these systems to inadvertently discriminate against certain groups or individuals must be carefully

considered and mitigated.

Another critical aspect of access control in the night-time economy is the interplay between technology and human interaction. While technology provides powerful tools for enhanced security, the human element remains crucial. Well-trained security personnel are essential for monitoring systems, responding to incidents, and making informed judgments in dynamic situations. A solely technological approach to access control would be inadequate, neglecting the critical role of human observation, judgment, and intervention, vital in ensuring the safety and security of both patrons and staff. The effective deployment of access control systems depends on the training, expertise, and ethical awareness of the security personnel who operate them. They must understand not only the technological aspects but also the legal and ethical implications of using such systems.

Proper training and oversight are crucial in ensuring that access control systems are used responsibly and in compliance with relevant laws and regulations.

The future of access control systems within the night-time economy lies in striking a delicate balance between

enhancing security and protecting individual rights and privacy. Technological innovation should always be

accompanied by ethical considerations and robust regulatory frameworks. Continuous development and refinement of access control systems, alongside the responsible training and deployment of security personnel, are essential for maintaining a safe and enjoyable environment for patrons while upholding the rights and freedoms of the public. The focus must always remain on using technology to enhance security in a manner that is both effective and ethical,

respecting the dignity and privacy of all individuals. This complex interplay between technology and human judgment will continue to shape the landscape of security in the years to come.

BodyWorn Cameras and Their Impact on Security Operations

The integration of body-worn cameras (BWCs) into the security operations of the night-time economy represents a significant technological shift, impacting not only the methods of evidence gathering but also the dynamics of interactions between security personnel and patrons. The adoption of BWCs has been driven by a confluence of factors, including a desire for increased accountability, improved evidence collection for legal proceedings, and the potential for de-escalation of potentially violent situations. However, the introduction of this technology is not without its complexities and challenges, raising concerns regarding privacy, data management, and the potential for unintended consequences.

One of the most significant benefits of BWCs is their ability to provide objective and verifiable evidence in the event of incidents. Historically, relying solely on the accounts of security personnel and witnesses has often led to conflicting narratives and difficulties in establishing the truth of events.

BWC footage provides an irrefutable record, significantly improving the accuracy and fairness of investigations into incidents such as assaults, theft, or allegations of misconduct against security staff. This objective evidence can be invaluable in supporting claims by security personnel, providing crucial context and detail that may otherwise be overlooked or contested. Moreover, the availability of this evidence can act as a deterrent against aggressive or disruptive behavior from patrons, knowing their actions are being recorded.

This enhanced accountability extends beyond the protection of security personnel. The use of BWCs can also help to hold patrons accountable for their actions. Instances of unruly behavior, verbal abuse, or physical altercations can be documented, providing irrefutable evidence for venue management to take appropriate action, such as issuing bans or pursuing legal avenues. This improved accountability across all stakeholders can contribute to a safer and more respectful environment within licensed premises. This isn't simply about penalizing individuals, but about creating a culture of responsibility and accountability that benefits everyone involved.

Furthermore, the presence of BWCs can, in many instances, act as a de-escalation tool. The knowledge that their actions are being recorded can often encourage patrons to modify their behavior, diffusing potentially volatile situations before they escalate into violence. The deterrent effect of the camera can be quite substantial, especially when combined with appropriate training for security personnel in conflict resolution and de-escalation techniques. Studies have shown that the mere visibility of BWCs can reduce the likelihood of aggressive behavior and promote a more respectful environment. However, it's crucial to acknowledge that this isn't a panacea; training remains paramount to effective de-escalation. A security officer simply activating a camera without proper communication and de-escalation skills could inadvertently inflame a situation.

The impact of BWCs extends beyond individual incidents; their use contributes to a broader improvement in data

collection for security management and analysis. Data

extracted from BWC footage can be used to identify patterns of behavior, hotspots for incidents, and even temporal trends in crime or disorder. This information can inform proactive security strategies, allowing venues to implement targeted interventions to enhance safety and prevent future incidents.

For example, by analyzing footage from multiple cameras and locations, management can identify times or days of the week that experience higher incident rates, allowing for adjusted staffing levels or enhanced security measures during those periods. This data-driven approach to security management is becoming increasingly vital in a world where efficient resource allocation and proactive crime prevention are paramount.

However, the implementation of BWCs is not without its challenges. One major concern revolves around privacy considerations. While BWCs are primarily intended to

record interactions relevant to security, there's a potential for the capture of incidental information pertaining to innocent bystanders. This raises ethical and legal questions about data protection, storage, and access. Strict guidelines and policies regarding data retention, access control, and the dissemination of information are absolutely crucial to mitigate these risks. Robust data protection protocols, including encryption and secure storage, are essential to prevent unauthorized access and safeguard the privacy of individuals unintentionally captured on camera.

Transparency about the BWC policy is also crucial,

informing patrons of their rights and the use of the footage.

The legal framework surrounding the use of BWCs in

security operations is also complex and varies considerably across jurisdictions. Clear legal guidelines are needed to define the circumstances under which BWC footage can be recorded, stored, accessed, and used as evidence. These guidelines must also address issues of data retention, ensuring that footage is only kept for a necessary period and securely deleted thereafter. Furthermore, the legal implications of using BWC footage in court proceedings must be clearly defined, including considerations for admissibility and the chain of custody. The lack of a clear, unified legal framework across the board can create inconsistencies and legal challenges.

The cost of implementing and maintaining a BWC system is another factor to consider. The initial investment in cameras, storage solutions, and data management software can be substantial, especially for larger venues or organizations.

Furthermore, ongoing costs related to equipment

maintenance, data storage, and staff training must also be factored in. This financial burden might be prohibitive for smaller venues, potentially creating disparities in security capabilities across the night-time economy. Cost-effectiveness analyses are crucial to assess the value proposition of BWCs relative to other security measures.

Finally, the effectiveness of BWCs is also dependent on the training and deployment of security personnel. Simply providing security officers with cameras without adequate training in their proper usage, data management protocols, and conflict de-escalation techniques is unlikely to yield the desired results. Comprehensive training programs are essential to ensure that BWCs are used appropriately and effectively, contributing to a safer and more accountable environment. This training should cover legal aspects,

privacy concerns, best practices for recording, and how to integrate BWC usage into overall security strategies. Regular refresher courses are also important to ensure that security personnel remain up-to-date with evolving best practices and legal requirements.

In conclusion, body-worn cameras represent a powerful tool in modern security operations within the night-time economy. Their potential benefits in terms of evidence gathering, accountability, and de-escalation are significant.

However, their implementation requires careful

consideration of ethical, legal, and practical challenges. A balanced approach that prioritizes both security and privacy, coupled with comprehensive training and robust data management protocols, is essential for realizing the full potential of BWCs while mitigating their potential drawbacks. The ongoing evolution of BWC technology and the accompanying legal and ethical frameworks will continue to shape the security landscape of the night-time economy for years to come. The future lies in a responsible and well-regulated implementation, ensuring this powerful technology is employed ethically and effectively to enhance safety and accountability for everyone involved.

Predictive Policing and Its Role in Security Planning

The integration of body-worn cameras marked a significant step in the technological evolution of nighttime security, but it's only one piece of a much larger, data-driven puzzle.

Predictive policing, the application of data analysis and algorithms to anticipate and prevent crime, is rapidly

reshaping the security landscape, including the challenges faced in the nightlife sector. This approach moves beyond reactive measures, aiming to proactively address potential threats before they escalate. The core principle is simple: by analyzing historical crime data, patterns of behavior, and various environmental factors, security teams can better allocate resources, deploy personnel strategically, and potentially intervene to prevent incidents before they occur.

However, the implementation of predictive policing in the context of the nighttime economy raises several complex questions. The data used to build these predictive models is crucial. Is the data representative of the diverse populations frequenting nightlife venues? Biases in the data, whether conscious or unconscious, can lead to skewed predictions, disproportionately targeting certain demographics or locations. For instance, if historical data reflects a higher incidence of incidents involving a particular age group or ethnicity, the algorithm might incorrectly predict future incidents involving that group, potentially leading to over-policing and discriminatory practices. This necessitates meticulous data cleansing and validation processes to ensure fairness and avoid perpetuating existing societal inequalities.

Furthermore, the accuracy of predictive models is constantly under scrutiny. While algorithms can identify trends and patterns, they cannot perfectly predict human behavior. Unforeseen circumstances, random events, and the inherent unpredictability of human interaction can render even the most sophisticated algorithms inaccurate. Over-reliance on predictive policing could lead to a false sense of security, potentially diverting resources from other crucial areas of security management. The effectiveness of predictive

policing must be continuously evaluated and adjusted based on real-world outcomes. Regular audits and feedback mechanisms are necessary to identify shortcomings and refine the models for improved accuracy and effectiveness.

Privacy concerns are another significant hurdle. The

collection and analysis of personal data for predictive

policing raise ethical questions about surveillance and the potential for misuse of information. Data privacy

regulations, such as GDPR in Europe and similar legislation elsewhere, must be strictly adhered to. Transparency is paramount; individuals should be informed about the types of data being collected, how it's being used, and who has access to it. The balance between effective security and the protection of individual rights is a delicate one, requiring careful consideration and robust safeguards. Implementing anonymization and data minimization techniques can help mitigate privacy risks without compromising the

effectiveness of predictive policing.

The integration of predictive policing also necessitates a shift in the mindset of security personnel. It's not simply about replacing human judgment with algorithms. Rather, it's about augmenting human capabilities with data-driven insights. Security personnel must be trained to interpret and utilize the output of predictive models effectively, understanding their limitations and avoiding bias in their application. This requires ongoing professional development and training programs to equip security officers with the necessary skills to work alongside technological advancements.

The use of predictive policing in the nightlife economy presents opportunities for improved resource allocation. By identifying high-risk times and locations, venues can deploy security staff more strategically, focusing their efforts where they are most needed. This can lead to more efficient use of resources, reducing costs and improving overall security effectiveness. For example, by analyzing data on incidents related to alcohol consumption and public disorder, venues can implement targeted strategies during peak hours or on specific days when risk is elevated. This might include increasing staff numbers, implementing stricter entry procedures, or coordinating with local law enforcement agencies for enhanced patrols.

Predictive policing also presents opportunities for proactive intervention. If a model identifies a potential for escalation in a particular area or situation, security personnel can intervene before an incident occurs. This might involve de-escalating a conflict, diverting potential troublemakers, or increasing visibility in a high-risk area. Early intervention can significantly reduce the severity of incidents and prevent escalation into violence. However, it's crucial to avoid preemptive actions based solely on predictive models.

Human judgment and a nuanced understanding of the

specific circumstances are essential to avoid

misinterpretations and potential for discriminatory or unjust practices. Such a proactive approach requires a highly skilled and trained security workforce capable of making sound judgments in complex and rapidly evolving situations.

Beyond the technological aspects, the successful

implementation of predictive policing hinges on collaboration and information sharing. Security personnel must work closely with law enforcement agencies, venue management, and local authorities to share data, coordinate strategies, and ensure a unified approach to security. Sharing data and insights can provide a more holistic understanding of crime patterns and allow for more effective interventions. However, data sharing must be governed by clear protocols and regulations to maintain privacy and prevent misuse of information.

The ethical considerations surrounding predictive policing are significant and multifaceted. Concerns about algorithmic bias, privacy violations, and the potential for discriminatory practices necessitate robust oversight and ethical guidelines.

Independent audits of predictive models are necessary to ensure fairness and accuracy, and regular evaluations of their impact on different communities are crucial to identify and mitigate any unintended consequences. Transparency in data collection and usage, along with robust mechanisms for redress and accountability, are essential for building public trust and ensuring the ethical deployment of predictive policing. Public discourse and engagement with affected communities are vital for establishing a shared understanding of both the benefits and potential drawbacks of these technologies.

Furthermore, the question of accountability is paramount. If predictive policing leads to miscarriages of justice or discriminatory outcomes, who is responsible? Clear lines of accountability must be established, and mechanisms for redress and appeal must be in place. This requires careful consideration of the legal and regulatory frameworks surrounding the use of predictive policing technologies and the development of transparent and accountable procedures for their implementation. It's not enough to simply deploy algorithms; there must be a system in place to address errors, correct biases, and ensure fairness and justice.

The future of security in the nightlife economy is

inextricably linked to the responsible development and

deployment of predictive policing. However, it's crucial to remember that technology is only one component of a

comprehensive security strategy. Human judgment, empathy, and effective training remain vital aspects of security work, especially in the complex and multifaceted environment of the nighttime economy. The most effective approach lies in finding a balance between leveraging the potential of data-driven insights and maintaining human oversight, ensuring that technology is used to enhance, not replace, the critical role of security personnel in keeping our communities safe. The human element, the understanding of local contexts, the ability to de-escalate volatile situations—these remain

irreplaceable aspects of effective security. The ideal outcome is a synergistic relationship between advanced technology and human expertise, creating a more effective and equitable security landscape for all. Ongoing research, ethical considerations, and open dialogue are crucial to ensuring that predictive policing is developed and implemented in a way that prioritizes both public safety and individual rights.

The Impact of Artificial Intelligence on Future Security

The integration of predictive policing, as discussed

previously, represents a significant leap forward in proactive security measures. However, the horizon extends far beyond this, reaching into the realm of artificial intelligence (AI), a technology poised to revolutionize how we approach safety and security, particularly within the dynamic environment of the night-time economy. The potential applications of AI are vast and transformative, promising to enhance existing security protocols and potentially address challenges

previously deemed insurmountable. Yet, this technological advancement is not without its ethical complexities and potential pitfalls, requiring careful consideration and responsible implementation.

One of the most discussed applications of AI in security is facial recognition technology. This system allows for the identification of individuals in real-time, potentially flagging known troublemakers or individuals banned from a venue.

Imagine a system that, upon entry, instantly compares a patron's face to a database of individuals with prior incidents of violence or disruptive behavior. Such a system could significantly reduce the likelihood of altercations and enhance the overall safety of patrons and staff. However, this technology is not without its concerns. Accuracy is paramount; false positives could lead to wrongful denial of entry, potentially creating legal issues and damaging the reputation of the venue. Moreover, the potential for misuse and the implications for privacy rights demand careful scrutiny. The ethical considerations around data collection, storage, and the potential for bias within the algorithms are critical to address before widespread adoption. Robust regulations and transparent oversight are absolutely vital to prevent abuse and protect civil liberties. The balance between enhanced security and individual rights remains a key challenge.

Beyond facial recognition, AI offers the potential to refine predictive analytics to an unprecedented degree. Instead of relying solely on historical crime data, AI algorithms can process vast quantities of information from diverse sources –social media sentiment, weather patterns, even real-time crowd density – to generate more nuanced and accurate predictions of potential trouble spots or high-risk times. This level of sophisticated analysis could allow security personnel to strategically allocate resources, preemptively address potential conflicts, and optimize staffing levels to match anticipated demand. For instance, AI could analyze historical data from a particular night to predict the likelihood of fights occurring on a given night and during particular hours. This allows for better resource allocation, such as additional security personnel during peak risk hours. The optimization of resource allocation extends to other areas, for instance, predicting the peak arrival and departure times, enabling better crowd management and smoother transitions. The potential to minimize wait times, streamline entry

procedures, and enhance the overall patron experience adds a significant business benefit to these security applications.

Automated threat detection is another area where AI

promises significant advancements. AI-powered systems can analyze video footage in real-time, identifying potential threats like weapons or suspicious behavior that might be missed by human observers. This is particularly valuable in crowded environments where immediate recognition of threats is crucial. For example, an AI system could be trained to recognize the distinctive features of a concealed weapon, alert security personnel instantly, and even provide real-time location data to enable rapid intervention. This capability can dramatically enhance the speed and

effectiveness of security responses, potentially mitigating the severity of dangerous situations. Furthermore, AI could analyze audio data to detect the escalating tones of a potential confrontation or the sounds associated with

violence, providing an early warning system for security personnel. The development and integration of such AI-powered surveillance systems would necessitate robust security protocols to prevent unauthorized access or

manipulation, along with strict ethical guidelines to ensure responsible data usage and protect against potential biases.

However, the implementation of AI in security is not without its obstacles. The initial investment costs for AI systems can be substantial, posing a challenge for smaller venues or those with limited budgets. Furthermore, the ongoing maintenance, updates, and training required to keep these systems functioning optimally add to the overall cost. This necessitates a careful cost-benefit analysis to ensure that the investment aligns with the potential returns in terms of improved safety and operational efficiency. The expertise required to operate and maintain these sophisticated systems is another key factor. Specialized training and ongoing professional development will be crucial for security personnel to effectively integrate AI tools into their daily work. This could require significant investment in education and training programs to ensure that security professionals are equipped with the skills necessary to utilize AI

technologies effectively.

Beyond the practical considerations, ethical concerns remain at the forefront of the AI discussion in security. Issues such as algorithmic bias, data privacy, and the potential for misuse of facial recognition technology are all significant challenges that must be addressed. Algorithmic bias, where AI systems discriminate against certain groups due to inherent biases in the data they are trained on, is a critical concern. For instance, if the training data used to develop a facial recognition system predominantly features individuals from one demographic group, the system may be less accurate when identifying individuals from other groups, potentially leading to unjust outcomes. This underlines the importance of diverse and representative datasets when training AI algorithms for security purposes. Moreover, ensuring data privacy and securing sensitive information are paramount.

Robust security measures are needed to protect against unauthorized access and prevent the misuse of collected data.

The potential for misuse of AI in security, such as targeted surveillance or the creation of predictive policing systems that disproportionately impact certain communities, also needs careful attention. Transparency and accountability mechanisms are necessary to prevent the abuse of this technology and safeguard fundamental rights. Therefore, the implementation of AI in security necessitates a collaborative approach, bringing together stakeholders from various sectors – security professionals, technologists, policymakers, and civil liberties advocates – to develop robust ethical guidelines and regulations. This collaborative process should prioritize responsible innovation, ensuring that AI is utilized to enhance safety and security while simultaneously protecting individual rights and freedoms. The ongoing dialogue and ethical debate surrounding the use of AI in security are essential to navigate the complex landscape of technological advancement and societal values. The aim should be a future where AI contributes to a safer, more equitable, and just night-time economy, not one where

technology exacerbates existing inequalities or infringes upon fundamental rights.

The future of security within the night-time economy is undeniably intertwined with the continued development and implementation of AI technologies. However, it's crucial to approach this technological evolution with a nuanced and responsible perspective. The human element, the on-the-ground experience, the ability to de-escalate tense situations, and the understanding of human behavior—these remain crucial components of effective security, regardless of technological advancements. The most effective security strategy will likely be one that leverages the power of AI to enhance human capabilities, rather than attempting to

replace human judgment and expertise entirely. This requires ongoing investment in training and education, not only to equip security professionals with the skills to utilize AI tools effectively, but also to cultivate critical thinking and ethical decision-making skills in the face of complex technological challenges. The responsible integration of AI in the security industry necessitates a commitment to transparency, accountability, and a continuous dialogue that prioritizes both public safety and the protection of individual rights.

Only through a cautious yet progressive approach can we harness the transformative potential of AI while mitigating the potential risks, creating a safer and more equitable night-time economy for all.

Securitys Impact on Public Safety in the NightTime Economy

The night-time economy, a vibrant tapestry woven from the threads of entertainment, hospitality, and social interaction, thrives on a delicate balance. Its success hinges not only on the allure of its offerings but also on the pervasive sense of safety and security it provides its patrons. This sense of security is not simply a matter of feeling safe; it's a tangible reality actively shaped and maintained by the often-unsung heroes of the night: security personnel. Their presence, their vigilance, and their proactive approach to potential threats are the unseen pillars supporting the thriving night-time economy. The impact extends far beyond simply preventing isolated incidents; it underpins the economic prosperity and social well-being of entire communities.

The contribution of security to public safety within the night-time economy is multifaceted. At its most basic level, it's about preventing crime. The visible presence of trained security personnel acts as a powerful deterrent to would-be offenders. Potential perpetrators, knowing they risk immediate confrontation and apprehension, are significantly less likely to engage in criminal activity. This preventative effect is particularly crucial in areas with high foot traffic and concentrations of alcohol consumption, where the potential for conflict and crime is naturally amplified.

Beyond deterrence, security personnel play a pivotal role in responding to incidents as they arise. Their training equips them to handle a range of situations, from minor disputes and unruly patrons to more serious incidents involving violence or theft. Their quick response, often crucial in the early stages of an incident, can significantly mitigate the severity of the outcome, preventing escalation and

minimizing harm. This immediate response capacity is frequently a lifesaver, particularly in situations where law enforcement may have a delayed arrival time. The ability to swiftly diffuse potentially volatile situations is a key skill possessed by trained security staff and contributes significantly to a safer environment for everyone.

Furthermore, security personnel contribute to a safer

environment through proactive measures. Regular patrols, proactive identification of potential trouble spots, and effective communication with staff and management allow them to anticipate and preempt potential problems before they escalate. This proactive approach is crucial in large venues or events where crowd management and security are paramount. By actively scanning for potential issues and responding swiftly, security personnel create a protective layer that significantly enhances public safety.

The impact of security extends beyond immediate incident prevention and response. It creates a climate of trust and confidence that is essential to the success of the night-time economy. Patrons are more likely to visit and spend money in areas where they feel safe and secure. Businesses, too, benefit from a safer environment, reducing the risk of property damage, theft, and reputational harm. This translates directly to increased profitability and economic stability for businesses operating within the night-time economy. The presence of security becomes an investment that yields substantial returns.

This positive impact is not limited to individual businesses; it extends to the broader economic health of communities. A vibrant and safe night-time economy attracts tourists, boosts local spending, and generates employment opportunities. It contributes to the overall economic vitality of the area, creating a positive feedback loop where increased safety leads to increased economic activity, which in turn fosters a further commitment to enhanced security measures. The economic benefits are substantial and reach far beyond the immediate revenue generated within the entertainment venues themselves. The ripple effect extends to neighboring businesses, accommodation providers, and the wider

community.

However, managing the night-time economy's security challenges isn't without its complexities. Large crowds, amplified by alcohol consumption, can present significant difficulties in crowd control. Security personnel need to employ sophisticated strategies to ensure smooth crowd flow, manage entry and exit points effectively, and respond appropriately to incidents within large crowds. This requires extensive training in crowd management techniques, effective communication strategies, and a deep understanding of human behavior in densely populated areas. The sheer scale of the challenge necessitates meticulous planning and coordination to ensure public safety.

Moreover, the security landscape within the night-time economy is constantly evolving. New threats emerge, technologies advance, and societal expectations shift.

Security professionals need to adapt continually to these changes, refining their approaches, adopting new

technologies, and refining their training to meet the ever-changing demands of their profession. This ongoing adaptation is crucial to maintaining the highest standards of public safety within the night-time economy.

Security's role in preventing and responding to violence is especially critical. Trained security personnel are often the first responders to incidents involving violence or aggression. Their capacity to de-escalate tense situations, mediate disputes, and, when necessary, restrain individuals, significantly reduces the likelihood of serious injury or escalation. Their proficiency in conflict resolution techniques, coupled with their ability to summon law enforcement assistance when needed, is an essential component of a safer night-time environment. This requires not just physical strength but also highly developed communication and de-escalation skills.

Finally, the social responsibility of security professionals extends beyond simply preventing crime and responding to incidents. They often act as guardians of the community, promoting responsible behavior and ensuring the well-being of patrons. Their interaction with the public creates opportunities for positive social engagement, contributing to a sense of community and shared responsibility for public safety. This social responsibility is often overlooked, yet it forms an integral part of the wider impact of security on the night-time economy.

In conclusion, the impact of security personnel on public safety within the night-time economy is undeniable. Their presence creates a safer environment, fostering economic growth and social well-being. From preventing crime through deterrence to responding swiftly and effectively to incidents, their contributions are multifaceted and far-reaching. As the night-time economy continues to evolve, the role of security professionals will remain crucial in safeguarding its vibrancy and ensuring the safety and well-being of all who participate in it. The ongoing adaptation and refinement of security strategies will be paramount in navigating the future challenges and maintaining a safer, more prosperous night-time economy for all.

The Economic Impact of a Safe NightTime Economy

The economic benefits of a secure night-time economy are substantial and far-reaching, extending beyond the

immediate revenue generated by bars, clubs, and restaurants.

A safe environment is a fundamental prerequisite for

attracting both visitors and businesses, fostering a climate of economic growth and stability. The presence of visible and effective security personnel acts as a powerful deterrent to crime, reducing incidents of theft, assault, and vandalism.

This, in turn, lowers insurance premiums for businesses, reducing operating costs and increasing profitability.

Businesses operating in a perceived safe environment are also more likely to attract investment, leading to expansion and job creation. A thriving night-time economy,

underpinned by robust security measures, stimulates the local economy through increased consumer spending, supporting ancillary businesses such as taxis, hotels, and restaurants. The knock-on effect on employment is significant, creating opportunities in security itself, but also in associated industries that benefit from increased footfall and activity.

Consider the impact on the hospitality sector. A reputation for safety and security is crucial for attracting tourists and attracting high-spending clientele. A single high-profile incident of violence or crime can severely damage a city's or town's reputation, deterring visitors and causing a ripple effect across the entire night-time economy. The subsequent loss of revenue can be substantial, impacting businesses, jobs, and local tax revenue. Conversely, a well-managed night-time economy, where safety is prioritized through visible and effective security, attracts tourists and encourages repeat visits, generating consistent revenue streams. This is particularly true for cities that actively promote their night-time offerings as a key part of their tourism strategy.

The role of security extends beyond simply preventing

crime. Well-trained security personnel can act as first

responders to incidents, providing immediate assistance and potentially preventing more serious consequences. Their presence can also provide reassurance to patrons,

encouraging them to spend more time and money in the area.

This increased dwell time benefits not just the immediate businesses but also those in the surrounding areas. A study conducted in a major UK city, for example, found a

significant correlation between the number of security

personnel deployed in a specific area and the overall increase in consumer spending during the evening and night hours.

The data showed a clear link between perceived safety and consumer confidence, with individuals feeling more

comfortable and willing to spend money in areas with visible security.

Furthermore, the presence of a strong security presence can contribute to the development of a positive brand image for a city or town. A reputation for safety attracts businesses that are seeking to establish themselves in a secure and stable market. This in turn leads to competition, innovation and a greater variety of services and entertainment options for consumers, all contributing to a more vibrant and economically prosperous night-time economy. The investment in security is, therefore, not just an expense, but a strategic investment with considerable returns. Cities with proactive and well-funded security strategies often see

higher levels of investment from both national and

international businesses. These businesses are seeking

locations with low crime rates, robust security measures, and a positive reputation for safety and order.

The economic benefits also extend beyond the immediate night-time economy. A safe and secure environment

encourages business owners to invest in upgrading their premises, improving infrastructure, and creating a more attractive environment for their customers. This can lead to wider regeneration and improvements in the surrounding areas, impacting daytime businesses and the community as a whole. The enhanced aesthetic appeal contributes to increased property values and attracts further investment, creating a virtuous cycle of economic growth. Consider, for instance, the revitalization of previously rundown docklands or industrial areas, where a well-managed night-time economy, supported by a robust security presence, has attracted new businesses, investment, and residents. These areas have become thriving hubs of activity, transforming the social and economic fabric of the surrounding communities.

However, the effectiveness of security measures is directly related to training, regulation, and ongoing professional development. Poorly trained security personnel can actually exacerbate problems, leading to negative interactions with patrons and potentially creating a sense of insecurity. This emphasizes the importance of rigorous training and ongoing professional development for security professionals. The Security Industry Authority (SIA) in the UK, for example, plays a crucial role in regulating the industry, ensuring that security personnel are properly licensed, trained, and vetted. This regulatory framework not only protects the public but also safeguards the reputation of the security industry itself.

A well-regulated industry inspires confidence among businesses and consumers alike, contributing to a more stable and economically robust night-time economy.

The economic impact of a safe night-time economy is demonstrably significant, extending far beyond the immediate revenue generated by venues and businesses. It involves attracting tourists, investment, fostering job creation, and improving the overall quality of life within a community. This positive impact is, however, dependent on a proactive approach to security, ensuring that trained and regulated security personnel are present and effective in their roles. Investing in security is, therefore, not merely a cost, but a strategic investment with a substantial return. It is an investment in the future economic prosperity and social well-being of the communities which rely on a vibrant and secure night-time economy.

The long-term economic sustainability of the night-time economy is intrinsically linked to the perception of safety and security. A city or town known for high levels of crime and disorder will struggle to attract visitors, businesses, and investment, hindering its economic growth. Conversely, a reputation for safety, built upon a visible and effective security presence, acts as a powerful magnet, attracting both tourists and businesses, creating a positive feedback loop of economic development. This is particularly crucial in the context of global competition, where cities are vying to attract tourists and businesses. A safe and well-managed night-time economy becomes a key differentiator, attracting both short-term revenue from tourism and longer-term investment and growth.

Moreover, the economic benefits extend beyond the

immediate commercial activity. A safe and vibrant night-time economy contributes to the overall quality of life within a community. It provides opportunities for social interaction, entertainment, and recreation, fostering a sense of community and belonging. This positive social atmosphere, underpinned by security, is attractive to residents, businesses, and potential investors. It promotes a sense of civic pride and contributes to the overall well-being of the community. The absence of crime and disorder allows residents to feel secure and enjoy their city or town's

amenities without fear. This is crucial in attracting families and young professionals, further contributing to the long-term economic sustainability of the area.

In conclusion, the economic impact of a safe and well-

managed night-time economy is undeniable and

multifaceted. From direct revenue generation to attracting investment and improving the overall quality of life, a secure environment is a critical catalyst for economic growth and prosperity. The role of security personnel in achieving this is paramount, requiring a commitment to training, regulation, and ongoing professional development. The investment in security is not merely a cost; it is a strategic investment that yields substantial returns, ensuring the long-term economic health and vibrancy of the night-time economy and the

communities it serves. As the night-time economy continues to evolve, the importance of security in its continued success and economic vitality will only increase. A proactive and comprehensive approach to security will be crucial in ensuring that the night-time economy continues to thrive, offering economic benefits and contributing to the social well-being of communities worldwide.

The Challenges of Managing Large Crowds and Events

The transition from a sparsely populated pub to a heaving nightclub, or a quiet festival field to a thronging concert venue, represents a dramatic shift in the demands placed on security personnel. The challenges inherent in managing large crowds are multifaceted, demanding a sophisticated blend of proactive planning, reactive problem-solving, and a deep understanding of crowd psychology. Effective crowd management isn't simply about preventing fights; it's about anticipating potential dangers, mitigating risks, and ensuring the smooth and safe flow of people. This requires more than just brute strength; it demands strategic thinking, communication skills, and a comprehensive understanding of relevant legislation and best practices.

One of the primary challenges lies in conducting a thorough risk assessment. This isn't a simple checklist but a dynamic process. It begins well before the event itself, considering the venue's layout, anticipated attendance, the type of event (a calm jazz concert presents different challenges than a high-energy rave), the historical incidents at similar events, and even the weather forecast. A meticulous risk assessment identifies potential flashpoints – areas prone to congestion, bottlenecks, or potential conflict – allowing security personnel to strategically deploy resources and implement preventative measures. For example, a narrow entranceway leading to a crowded dance floor might require additional staff to manage the flow of people, preventing dangerous overcrowding. Similarly, identifying potential escape routes and ensuring they are clearly marked and unobstructed is crucial for swift and safe evacuation in emergencies. The assessment also considers the potential for alcohol-fuelled aggression, drug use, or even acts of terrorism, requiring the development of robust contingency plans. These plans aren't merely theoretical exercises; they are meticulously rehearsed, ensuring that security teams are well-prepared to respond effectively and efficiently to a range of scenarios.

Once the risk assessment is complete, the deployment of security personnel becomes crucial. This is not simply about distributing staff evenly across the venue; it involves placing experienced personnel in critical areas identified during the risk assessment. A skilled supervisor, experienced in crowd psychology and conflict resolution, is more valuable at a potential flashpoint than a less experienced individual in a quieter area. Effective communication between security personnel is equally important; radio systems, clear signaling, and established communication protocols are essential for rapid response and coordinated action. The use of CCTV and other surveillance technologies can also significantly enhance the overall situational awareness of the security team, allowing them to monitor crowd density, identify potential troublemakers, and respond quickly to any incidents.

Crowd control itself requires a blend of preventative and reactive measures. Preventative measures involve controlling access, managing the flow of people, and establishing clear boundaries. This might include using barriers, queuing systems, and designated entry and exit points. A well-planned queuing system can drastically reduce the risk of bottlenecks and congestion, while clear signage and the effective use of marshals can guide the movement of people in a safe and orderly manner. Effective communication with the public is also crucial; clear instructions, politely given, can significantly enhance cooperation and reduce the likelihood of incidents. However, even with the best

preventative measures, incidents can occur. Therefore,

reactive crowd control strategies are essential. This involves being well-equipped to handle aggression, substance misuse, and medical emergencies. Training in conflict resolution, first aid, and appropriate use of force is essential for all security personnel involved in crowd management. The ability to calmly de-escalate volatile situations is often more effective than resorting to physical intervention. A calm, assertive approach, coupled with clear communication, can often defuse tense situations before they escalate.

The legal framework within which security personnel

operate is also a critical consideration. The use of force must be proportionate, justified, and within the bounds of the law.

Excessive force can lead to serious legal consequences for both the individual officer and the company they work for.

Similarly, understanding the rights of individuals under arrest or detention is crucial, ensuring that procedures are followed correctly and that the rights of the public are respected. Regular training and updates on relevant

legislation are therefore essential to maintain compliance and minimise legal risks.

Furthermore, effective post-event analysis is vital. This involves reviewing incident reports, CCTV footage, and feedback from staff and patrons to identify areas for

improvement. Were there any unforeseen challenges? Could security protocols have been more effective? What lessons can be learned for future events? This continuous cycle of improvement is essential for maintaining high standards of crowd safety and minimizing the risk of future incidents. The night-time economy thrives on its vibrant social life, but that vibrancy is dependent upon the seamless and safe management of large gatherings. The role of security personnel in this process is not merely a reactive one; it is proactive, demanding meticulous planning, skilled execution, and a constant commitment to enhancing safety and security for all.

The use of technology is increasingly crucial in managing large crowds. Advanced CCTV systems, with facial

recognition capabilities, can be used to monitor crowd

density, identify potential troublemakers, and provide real-time information to security personnel. Body-worn cameras can provide evidence in case of incidents and also act as a deterrent to anti-social behavior. Radio communication systems allow for instant communication between different security teams, enabling a rapid and coordinated response to emergencies. Even the use of social media monitoring can be beneficial, allowing security teams to identify and address potential issues before they escalate. However, the effective use of technology requires careful consideration of data privacy and ethical implications. The collection and use of personal data must be compliant with relevant regulations, ensuring the balance between security and individual rights.

Beyond the technological advancements, the human element remains paramount. The training and development of security personnel are critical in mitigating risks and ensuring the safety of event attendees. Effective training should cover a wide range of topics, including crowd psychology, conflict resolution, first aid, communication skills, legal frameworks, and the appropriate use of force.

Regular refresher courses and ongoing professional

development are essential to maintain high standards of competence and to keep security personnel up-to-date with the latest best practices and technological advancements.

Furthermore, fostering a culture of teamwork and

communication within the security team is crucial for effective collaboration and coordinated responses to

incidents. Regular team briefings and debriefings, coupled with opportunities for feedback and improvement, can strengthen team cohesion and ensure that everyone is working towards the common goal of ensuring public safety.

The economic consequences of poor crowd management are substantial. A poorly managed event can lead to injuries, property damage, and even fatalities. Such incidents can result in substantial legal costs, reputational damage, and a loss of future business. The financial implications of inadequate security measures are far-reaching, encompassing insurance claims, legal fees, lost revenue, and potential fines for non-compliance with safety regulations. Conversely, a well-managed event, with robust security protocols in place, can foster a sense of trust and safety amongst patrons,

enhancing their experience and encouraging repeat business. This positive reputation can translate into increased revenue and long-term economic success for venues and event organizers. The investment in effective crowd management is therefore not merely a cost; it is a strategic investment that protects both the financial and reputational integrity of the organization and ensures the long-term sustainability of the night-time economy. Investing in training, technology, and skilled personnel is a crucial element in promoting a safe and vibrant night-time environment, fostering economic

prosperity and ensuring the well-being of all stakeholders. The seemingly mundane task of crowd control is, in reality, a complex endeavor requiring a sophisticated blend of planning, technology, and human expertise, all working in harmony to ensure the safety and enjoyment of patrons within the vibrant context of the night-time economy.

Securitys Role in Preventing and Responding to Violence

The effectiveness of security personnel in mitigating

violence within the night-time economy hinges not only on their physical presence but, crucially, on their training and preparedness. The days of simply ejecting troublemakers are long gone. Modern security professionals are increasingly trained in conflict resolution, de-escalation techniques, and communication strategies designed to prevent violence before it erupts. This shift reflects a broader societal understanding of the complexities of aggression and the importance of proactive intervention. Effective de-escalation isn't about passively waiting for a situation to worsen; it's about actively identifying potential flashpoints,

understanding the dynamics of conflict, and employing a range of communication skills to diffuse tense situations.

This training often involves role-playing scenarios,

simulating common conflicts encountered in the night-time economy. Door supervisors learn to identify verbal and non-verbal cues that signal escalating tension, such as raised voices, aggressive body language, or the consumption of excessive alcohol. The training emphasizes empathy and active listening, encouraging security personnel to understand the perspectives of individuals involved in disputes and to address their concerns calmly and rationally.

De-escalation techniques are not about appeasement; they are about strategically managing conflict, creating space for rational dialogue, and diffusing potentially volatile situations before they escalate into physical violence.

A significant component of modern security training focuses on understanding the psychology of aggression. Security professionals are taught to recognize the triggers that can lead to violence, such as perceived threats, personal insults, or alcohol-fueled aggression. They learn to identify individuals who may be prone to violence and to implement strategies to prevent interactions that could lead to conflict.

This proactive approach is vital in preventing violence before it has a chance to escalate. It requires astute

observation, quick thinking, and the ability to anticipate potential problems. In crowded environments, the ability to identify potential hotspots and position staff accordingly is critical. This involves understanding crowd dynamics, anticipating potential choke points, and deploying personnel strategically to manage the flow of people and prevent bottlenecks that could contribute to tension and aggression.

Furthermore, effective security in the night-time economy relies on strong collaboration with law enforcement agencies. This partnership is essential for dealing with serious incidents, responding to emergencies, and sharing intelligence about known troublemakers or potential threats.

Regular liaison with local police forces enables security teams to receive updates on ongoing issues and to share information about individuals who may pose a risk to public safety. This collaboration streamlines responses to incidents, ensuring swift and effective action in situations demanding immediate attention. Effective communication between security personnel and law enforcement is vital in these situations, ensuring that information is passed on accurately and efficiently.

The role of technology in violence prevention is also

increasingly significant. CCTV systems provide invaluable evidence in the event of an incident, allowing for identification of perpetrators and the reconstruction of events. They also act as a deterrent, reducing the likelihood of violent behaviour. Modern CCTV systems are sophisticated, offering high-resolution imagery and advanced analytical capabilities, such as facial recognition software and crowd monitoring tools. This enables security personnel to monitor large areas effectively, identifying potential threats and responding swiftly to any incidents. The use of body-worn cameras by security personnel is becoming increasingly commonplace, providing further protection for both security staff and members of the public, offering

irrefutable evidence in case of disputes.

The legal framework surrounding the use of force by security personnel is also a critical aspect of training and operational procedures. Security professionals must understand the limits of their powers and the legal consequences of exceeding those limits. They need to be thoroughly trained in the appropriate use of restraint techniques, prioritizing safety and minimizing the risk of injury to both themselves and those they are dealing with.

This often involves specific training in self-defense

techniques, but with a strong emphasis on de-escalation and only using force as a last resort. The legal ramifications of using excessive force are significant, ranging from civil lawsuits to criminal prosecution.

Beyond the immediate response to violence, the role of security extends to post-incident management. This involves collecting evidence, providing statements to the police, and liaising with other relevant stakeholders, such as venue management and emergency services. Security personnel are often the first point of contact for victims of violence or crime, and their ability to provide immediate support and care is crucial. This requires training in basic first aid and the ability to calm and reassure individuals who have experienced traumatic events. The post-incident management process includes thorough reporting and analysis of the incident to prevent similar events in the future. This involves identifying contributing factors, assessing the effectiveness of security measures, and implementing improvements to security procedures.

The effectiveness of security's role in preventing and

responding to violence is also dependent on the overall

environment in which security operates. A well-managed venue, with clear signage, adequate lighting, and a

responsible approach to alcohol service, can significantly reduce the likelihood of violent incidents. The cooperation of venue management is essential in creating a safe and secure environment. It's a shared responsibility between the venue and the security team; the effectiveness of the security measures will be directly linked to the level of support provided by management in terms of resources, training, and policy implementation.

The economic impact of effective violence prevention

cannot be overstated. A safe and secure night-time economy attracts patrons, encouraging repeat visits and boosting the profitability of businesses. A reputation for safety encourages investment, supporting growth and job creation within the sector. Conversely, a reputation for violence can deter customers, leading to decreased revenue and economic hardship for venues and businesses in the surrounding area. The cost of violence extends beyond the immediate financial losses; it can encompass the costs associated with legal fees, insurance claims, and reputational damage. This highlights the importance of robust security measures as a vital

investment protecting both the immediate economic interests of venues and the long-term sustainability of the night-time economy as a whole. The economic benefits associated with preventing violence extend beyond the immediate financial gains; they contribute to the wider social wellbeing of the community, promoting a sense of safety and security that benefits everyone.

Furthermore, the training and professionalism of security personnel directly impact public perception. A well-trained and courteous security team can enhance the overall experience for patrons, fostering a positive atmosphere and contributing to the vibrancy of the night-time economy. This contributes to a positive brand image for venues and businesses, attracting more customers and supporting economic growth. The commitment to high standards of professionalism and customer service demonstrates a commitment to safety and customer satisfaction, ultimately benefitting the whole industry. The reputation of professionalism transcends the immediate impact on the night-time economy; it builds public trust in the security industry and strengthens its position as a vital component of a thriving, safe, and secure community. The long-term economic and social benefits extend far beyond the individual venues and businesses; they reflect a commitment to public safety and a better quality of life for all.

The Social Responsibility of Security Professionals

The previous section highlighted the crucial role of training and professionalism in enhancing the effectiveness of security personnel. However, the responsibilities of those working in the night-time economy extend far beyond simply preventing violence or managing unruly patrons. A significant and often overlooked aspect of their work is the inherent social responsibility they carry, a responsibility that impacts not only the immediate environment of the venue but also the broader community. This social responsibility encompasses several key areas: promoting responsible alcohol consumption, fostering a safe and inclusive

environment, engaging with local communities, and acting as responsible citizens within the night-time economy.

One of the most prominent aspects of this social

responsibility lies in the management of alcohol

consumption. Security personnel are often the first line of defense against excessive drinking and its associated

problems. Their role is not merely to stop intoxicated

individuals from entering a premises, but also to actively promote responsible behavior. This involves identifying and addressing signs of intoxication early, encouraging patrons to pace their drinking, and intervening when necessary to prevent potential harm. This proactive approach requires a nuanced understanding of alcohol's effects, the ability to communicate effectively with intoxicated individuals, and the judgment to know when to escalate an intervention to other staff or emergency services. Furthermore, this responsibility extends beyond individual patrons. Security staff play a critical role in maintaining order and preventing situations where large groups engage in excessive drinking, leading to public disorder or violence. By employing de-escalation techniques, proactively addressing disruptive behavior, and collaborating with venue management to implement responsible serving policies, security professionals can significantly reduce alcohol-related problems within the night-time economy.

Beyond alcohol management, security professionals

contribute significantly to creating a safe and inclusive

environment for all patrons. This requires a commitment to inclusivity and a zero-tolerance policy towards

discrimination of any kind. Security personnel are often the first point of contact for individuals who may feel harassed, threatened, or unsafe. Their response to such situations significantly influences a patron's experience and can determine whether a venue is perceived as welcoming and safe. Training in diversity awareness, conflict resolution, and appropriate responses to incidents of harassment is crucial. This extends to the awareness and responsible management of vulnerable individuals, those under the influence of drugs or alcohol, or those experiencing mental health crises.

Effective security requires understanding the complexities of these situations and employing strategies that prioritize safety and dignity. This includes knowing when and how to engage with emergency services, when to seek medical assistance, and when to de-escalate a situation without compromising safety. The ability to calmly and compassionately handle these situations creates a safer and more respectful environment for all patrons.

The social responsibility of security professionals extends beyond the walls of the venues they protect. Active engagement with the local community is paramount.

Building positive relationships with local residents,

businesses, and law enforcement agencies is essential for fostering a collaborative approach to managing the night-time economy. This collaboration might involve participation in community forums, attending local meetings, or working with neighbourhood watch schemes to address concerns about noise, disorder, or anti-social behavior. Open communication and a willingness to address community concerns can greatly improve the relationship between the night-time economy and local residents, fostering mutual respect and understanding. This collaborative approach minimizes potential conflicts and promotes a sense of shared responsibility for the well-being of the community.

Furthermore, security personnel can play a vital role in reporting crime or suspicious activities to the appropriate authorities. This contributes to community safety and helps law enforcement agencies maintain order and prevent crime.

Moreover, the social responsibility of security professionals encompasses their conduct and behavior both on and off duty. They act as representatives of the security industry, and their actions have a direct impact on the public's perception of the profession. Maintaining high ethical standards, demonstrating integrity, and upholding the law are essential aspects of their social responsibility. This commitment to professionalism reinforces public trust in the security industry and supports the industry's efforts to improve its image and reputation. This includes a commitment to

adhering to the regulations and guidelines set by the Security Industry Authority (SIA) and maintaining a professional demeanour at all times. This demonstrates a commitment to public safety and a commitment to upholding the highest standards of conduct within the profession. By being responsible citizens and acting with integrity, security professionals contribute to building a more positive perception of the night-time economy and fostering a stronger sense of community.

The social responsibility of security professionals in the night-time economy is multifaceted and extends far beyond the basic responsibilities of maintaining order and preventing violence. It requires a sophisticated understanding of social dynamics, conflict resolution, community engagement, and ethical conduct. Training programs must therefore encompass a broader curriculum that goes beyond physical skills and incorporates these essential social elements. The training needs to instill a deep sense of responsibility and empower security personnel to act as positive role models and agents of change within their communities. This requires a dedicated approach by training providers, venue managers, and licensing authorities, and requires consistent investment in the development of professional competencies. This integrated approach will ensure that security professionals are not just responsible for managing risk, but also for actively contributing to the social well-being of the night-time economy and the communities they serve. The long-term benefits are substantial: a safer, more inclusive, and more vibrant night-time economy, where the security

industry is viewed not just as a necessary component, but as an active partner in building strong, thriving communities.

Furthermore, the social responsibility of security

professionals shouldn't be seen as an added burden, but rather as an integral part of their job description. It's a

recognition of the crucial role they play in shaping the

environment within which they operate. By actively

promoting responsible behavior, fostering inclusivity,

engaging with local communities, and acting with integrity, security professionals can dramatically improve the quality of life for everyone involved in the night-time economy. This is not simply a matter of ethical conduct; it's a matter of effective risk management. By building strong relationships with the communities they serve, security personnel can better anticipate and address potential problems, reducing the likelihood of conflicts and improving the overall safety and security of the night-time economy. This proactive approach to social responsibility is not only beneficial for the communities themselves but is also good business for venues and companies. A safer and more welcoming environment attracts more customers and contributes to the economic prosperity of the night-time economy. In conclusion, the social responsibility of security professionals is not just a moral imperative, but also a crucial component of a successful and sustainable night-time economy.

The evolving nature of the night-time economy also

demands a constantly evolving understanding of social

responsibility. With the rise of new technologies, changing social norms, and the emergence of new challenges, security professionals must continuously adapt and refine their approaches. This requires ongoing training, professional development, and a commitment to staying informed about best practices. Regular updates on legislation, effective conflict resolution techniques, and awareness of diverse cultural sensitivities are essential components of this ongoing development. The industry needs to actively embrace initiatives that promote professional development and encourage security personnel to engage in reflective practice, ensuring their practices remain current and relevant.

The ongoing investment in training and development will not only benefit individual security professionals, but will also improve the overall effectiveness and social

responsibility of the entire security industry. This investment should also extend to research into the most effective strategies for promoting responsible behavior, reducing crime, and fostering positive community relationships. This evidence-based approach will help to ensure that the social responsibility initiatives are effective and adaptable to the changing needs of the night-time economy.

Finally, it's crucial to acknowledge the often challenging and demanding nature of the work. Security professionals frequently face difficult situations, confrontational

individuals, and stressful environments. Recognizing the emotional toll of this work is vital and providing access to appropriate support services, such as counseling and stress management programs, is crucial for the well-being of security personnel. This support is not merely a matter of compassion; it's also a matter of promoting professionalism and effectiveness. Burnout and stress can significantly impact the performance and judgment of security professionals, potentially compromising their ability to effectively carry out their social responsibilities. By providing appropriate support and resources, the industry can ensure that security professionals are well-equipped to handle the demands of their jobs and contribute positively to the night-time economy and the broader community. This investment in the well-being of security personnel is a crucial component of promoting a responsible, ethical, and effective security industry. The long-term benefits of this approach will be a more resilient, professional, and socially responsible security workforce, equipped to meet the challenges and opportunities of the ever-evolving night-time economy.

Analysis of Successful Security Strategies in Different Venues

This section delves into the practical application of security strategies across diverse venues within the night-time economy. We will examine successful models, analyze their key components, and extract valuable lessons learned for improving security effectiveness and promoting a safer environment for patrons and staff alike. The case studies presented here are drawn from real-world examples, highlighting both the successes and, where appropriate, the areas for improvement. Understanding these diverse approaches is crucial for anyone involved in security management, allowing for adaptation and optimization of strategies based on specific venue requirements and potential threats.

One compelling example comes from the "The Roxy," a large, multi-room nightclub in a major city. Their security strategy revolves around a layered approach, starting with robust external security measures. This includes highly visible door supervisors, strategically placed CCTV cameras with live monitoring, and a well-defined entry and exit system to manage crowd flow efficiently. Internal security incorporates a team of roving patrols, trained in conflict de-escalation and crowd control, equipped with body-worn cameras for evidence gathering and accountability.

Furthermore, The Roxy utilizes sophisticated access control systems, including RFID wristbands linked to a central database, allowing for better tracking of patrons and immediate identification of any individuals causing issues. Their success stems from a proactive approach, prioritizing prevention through a strong visible presence and efficient crowd management. They also actively foster a positive relationship with local law enforcement, facilitating rapid response in the event of emergencies.

In stark contrast, a smaller, independent pub called "The Old Smithy" relies on a more personalized, community-focused approach. Given its smaller size and more intimate atmosphere, The Old Smithy's security strategy emphasizes knowing their regular clientele and fostering a sense of community responsibility. While they employ a door supervisor during peak hours, the focus is less on overt security measures and more on creating a welcoming, yet safe environment. The owner and staff actively engage with patrons, encouraging responsible alcohol consumption and proactively addressing any potential conflicts before they escalate. Their success lies in building trust and creating a culture of mutual respect, making the pub a safe and enjoyable space for locals. This approach emphasizes proactive engagement and a personalized touch, demonstrating that security doesn't always require heavy-handed tactics.

Moving beyond traditional pubs and nightclubs, let's

examine the security strategies employed at large-scale outdoor music festivals. Festival security requires a highly coordinated and multi-faceted approach, often involving collaboration between multiple security firms, law enforcement agencies, and event organizers. A successful example is the "Summer Sounds" festival, which prioritizes advanced planning and risk assessment. They employ a comprehensive security plan addressing potential threats such as overcrowding, substance abuse, and potential terrorist attacks. Their strategy involves a layered approach, with external perimeter security, internal patrols, and a dedicated team managing crowd flow and entry/exit points.

Advanced technology, including drone surveillance for monitoring large crowds and real-time communication systems for rapid response to incidents, plays a significant role. The success of Summer Sounds underscores the importance of detailed planning, proactive risk mitigation, and seamless coordination between various security personnel and external agencies.

However, it's equally important to examine instances where security strategies have fallen short. A review of security failures provides valuable lessons for improving future practices. One such example involves a nightclub that experience a major incident due to inadequate crowd control measures. The club lacked a clear evacuation plan, leading to chaos and injuries during an unexpected emergency. Their CCTV system was outdated and ineffective, hindering investigations. This case highlights the critical need for comprehensive emergency plans, regular security audits, and investment in modern, reliable technology. A thorough post-incident review is crucial for learning from mistakes and implementing corrective actions to prevent similar incidents in the future.

Another instructive case involves a pub that experienced a series of assaults due to poor staff training and inadequate conflict resolution protocols. The door supervisors lacked appropriate de-escalation techniques and failed to effectively manage aggressive patrons. This exemplifies the necessity of investing in comprehensive staff training, emphasizing conflict de-escalation, communication skills, and appropriate use of force. Regular refresher courses and ongoing professional development are vital for maintaining security staff competence.

These case studies illustrate the multifaceted nature of successful security strategies. There is no one-size-fits-all solution, and the optimal approach is heavily dependent on the specific venue, its clientele, and the potential threats.

However, several common threads emerge: proactive risk assessment and planning, effective staff training, utilization of appropriate technology, and a willingness to learn from past mistakes are crucial elements.

Successful strategies often prioritize prevention over

reaction, employing measures to deter incidents before they occur. This may involve visible security presence, clear communication with patrons, and a well-defined set of rules and regulations. Effective communication is crucial, both within the security team and between security personnel and patrons. Clear signage, announcements, and proactive engagement with the crowd can significantly reduce the likelihood of incidents.

The use of technology, while not a panacea, can significantly enhance security effectiveness. CCTV systems, access control systems, and body-worn cameras can provide valuable evidence, deter criminal activity, and enhance accountability. However, it's essential to balance the use of technology with privacy considerations and ethical implications.

Finally, collaboration is key. Effective security strategies often involve close collaboration between security personnel, venue management, local law enforcement agencies, and other stakeholders. This fosters a coordinated response to potential threats and improves overall safety. Regular communication and joint training exercises can enhance preparedness and coordination.

In conclusion, analyzing successful security strategies

requires a comprehensive understanding of the specific context. However, common best practices emerge that transcend venue-specific differences. By understanding these best practices and learning from past failures, security professionals can create safer and more enjoyable

environments within the night-time economy. The examples provided in this chapter are not exhaustive but offer a representative sample of successful and unsuccessful security strategies, providing valuable insights for those aiming to improve their own approach to security management. Furthermore, continued research and adaptation to evolving threats and technologies will remain crucial in maintaining high levels of safety and security within the diverse venues that comprise the vibrant landscape of the night-time economy. The future of security relies on a dynamic and adaptive approach, constantly evolving to meet the challenges of a changing world.

Examining Incidents and Lessons Learned from Security Failures

This section shifts focus from successful security strategies to examining incidents where security measures fell short, leading to undesirable consequences. Analyzing these failures offers invaluable lessons, highlighting critical areas for improvement in training, planning, and operational procedures within the night-time economy. Understanding these shortcomings is as crucial, if not more so, than

understanding successes, as it allows for proactive risk mitigation and the development of more robust security protocols.

One prominent example involves a large nightclub in a major city. While boasting state-of-the-art surveillance technology and a seemingly adequate number of door supervisors, a serious incident occurred involving a large-scale brawl that resulted in multiple injuries and significant property damage. Investigation revealed several critical weaknesses. Firstly, the door supervisors, while possessing SIA licenses, lacked sufficient training in crowd management techniques and de-escalation strategies. Their response to the escalating conflict was reactive rather than proactive, allowing the situation to spiral out of control before adequate intervention could be implemented.

Secondly, despite the advanced surveillance system, the footage proved difficult to analyze in real-time due to a lack of adequately trained personnel monitoring the feeds and a cumbersome system interface. The delay in identifying the escalating threat contributed significantly to the severity of the incident. Finally, communication between the door team and internal security personnel, as well as with local law enforcement, proved to be inefficient and fragmented. This lack of coordination hampered a swift and effective response.

This case highlights the crucial interplay between

technology, personnel training, and effective communication.

Technological advancements, while beneficial, are only as effective as the people who operate and interpret them. The nightclub's failure stemmed not from a lack of resources, but from a lack of integration and a failure to invest adequately in comprehensive training for its security personnel. The incident underscores the need for regular refresher courses focusing on practical skills, including de-escalation techniques, conflict resolution, and effective communication strategies. Furthermore, it underscores the need for clear protocols on escalation procedures, outlining specific roles and responsibilities for different members of the security team and establishing seamless communication channels with external agencies.

Another illustrative case involves a smaller pub experiencing a series of petty thefts and instances of vandalism. While the pub employed a single door supervisor, their efforts were primarily focused on managing entry and exit, leaving the interior vulnerable. The lack of regular internal patrols and insufficient security measures such as adequate CCTV

coverage allowed these incidents to occur repeatedly. This case exemplifies the importance of adapting security

strategies to the specific context of the venue. A smaller establishment may not require the same level of

technological sophistication as a large nightclub, but a

comprehensive risk assessment and a tailored security plan, including regular internal patrols and visible security measures, are crucial regardless of size. The pub's failure highlights the vulnerability of understaffed and inadequately trained security teams, even in smaller venues.

A different scenario involves a concert venue that

experienced a significant overcrowding incident. Although the venue had a capacity limit, inadequate crowd control measures at entry points and a lack of effective crowd flow management within the venue itself led to a dangerous situation. Poor communication between the venue management, security personnel, and event organizers further exacerbated the problem. This incident emphasizes the importance of careful planning and coordination in high-density environments. A robust crowd management plan, including clearly defined entry and exit routes, designated crowd control personnel, and the use of appropriate technology to monitor crowd density in real-time, is paramount. Collaboration between all stakeholders is critical to ensure that plans are effectively executed and adjusted as needed. The failure in this case underscores the need for regular training specific to crowd control techniques,

including crowd dynamics, safe dispersal strategies, and understanding the potential hazards of overcrowding.

These examples showcase the variety of security challenges faced within the night-time economy, emphasizing that a one-size-fits-all approach is insufficient. Effective security relies on a comprehensive understanding of the specific threats and vulnerabilities present in each unique environment. This understanding must inform a detailed security plan that addresses potential risks proactively. Such a plan should consider:

Risk Assessment:

A thorough assessment identifying potential risks, vulnerabilities, and threats specific to the venue and its clientele. This should consider factors such as location, type of establishment, opening hours, and the demographic profile of its patrons.

Staff Training:

Comprehensive training programs for all security personnel, incorporating practical skills in crowd management, conflict resolution, de-escalation, first aid, and the use of any security technology employed. Regular

refresher courses are essential to maintain proficiency and update personnel on best practices and emerging threats.

Technology Integration:

Strategic implementation of security technology, chosen to address specific needs and vulnerabilities identified in the risk assessment. This might include CCTV systems, access control systems, metal detectors, or other relevant technologies. Crucially, this technology should be integrated effectively and monitored by adequately trained personnel.

Communication Protocols:

Establishing clear communication protocols between all stakeholders, including security personnel, venue management, event organizers, and local law enforcement. Efficient communication is critical for swift and effective response to incidents.

Emergency Response Planning:

Developing and regularly rehearsing comprehensive emergency response plans to address various scenarios, including medical emergencies, violence, and fire. These plans should incorporate clear procedures for evacuation, communication, and coordination with emergency services.

Regular Review and Adaptation:

Continuously reviewing and adapting the security plan in response to feedback, incident reports, and evolving security threats. Regular audits of security procedures are vital to ensure their ongoing effectiveness.

The common thread linking these case studies is a failure to appreciate the holistic nature of security. It's not merely about the presence of security personnel or the deployment of technology; it's about the integration of these elements within a well-defined, comprehensive security plan that is proactively managed, regularly reviewed, and adapted to changing circumstances. The lessons learned from these failures highlight the importance of investing in proper training, fostering effective communication, and understanding that security is a continuous process requiring ongoing vigilance and adaptation. Neglecting these crucial elements can have serious consequences, ranging from

minor property damage to serious injury or even fatality. By learning from past mistakes, the night-time economy can create safer and more enjoyable environments for everyone. The ultimate goal is not just to prevent incidents but to create a culture of proactive safety where all stakeholders work collaboratively to mitigate risks and ensure a positive experience for all. The ongoing evolution of the security industry requires constant learning, adaptation, and a commitment to providing the highest standards of protection.

Best Practices for Conflict Resolution and Deescalation

Building upon the lessons learned from past security failures, effective conflict resolution and de-escalation are paramount to maintaining order and safety within the night-time economy. These skills are not merely supplementary to physical security measures; they are fundamental components of a comprehensive approach, often preventing incidents before they escalate into violence or require physical intervention. Proactive de-escalation can transform a potentially volatile situation into a calm and controlled environment, protecting both patrons and staff.

The cornerstone of effective de-escalation lies in verbal communication. A security professional's ability to calmly and confidently address individuals exhibiting aggressive or disruptive behavior is crucial. This requires more than just clear articulation; it demands active listening, empathy, and a nuanced understanding of human behavior. Understanding the underlying causes of conflict – be it intoxication, personal disputes, or pre-existing aggression – is vital in tailoring a response. A blanket approach rarely works; each situation requires a unique strategy.

For instance, an individual heavily intoxicated and verbally abusive may require a different approach than someone involved in a heated argument with a friend. The intoxicated individual might respond better to calm, reassuring language and a slower, more deliberate pace of communication.

Conversely, those engaged in a personal dispute may require a more structured intervention, facilitating a conversation aimed at finding common ground or separating them before the situation worsens.

Effective communication necessitates clear and concise language, avoiding jargon or overly authoritative tones. Using "I" statements instead of accusatory "you" statements can significantly de-escalate tension. For example, instead of saying, "You're being disruptive and need to calm down," a more effective approach might be, "I'm noticing that the volume of your conversation is escalating, and I'm concerned it might upset other patrons." This approach acknowledges the individual's behavior without directly attacking them, creating space for dialogue.

Non-verbal communication is equally important.

Maintaining a calm and open posture, making appropriate eye contact (without being overly confrontational), and mirroring the individual's body language (to a certain extent) can build rapport and foster understanding. Conversely, aggressive body language, such as crossing arms or standing in a threatening stance, will almost certainly escalate the situation. Maintaining personal space while ensuring a clear line of sight is also vital; this avoids appearing either overly aggressive or dismissive.

Training in de-escalation techniques is not simply about memorizing phrases; it involves developing a heightened sense of situational awareness and emotional intelligence. Security personnel should be trained to recognize warning signs of escalating conflict, such as clenched fists, raised voices, or increasingly aggressive body language. Early intervention, even before a conflict overtly begins, is often the most effective strategy. This may involve separating potentially problematic individuals or redirecting their attention to a less stressful activity.

A crucial aspect often overlooked is the importance of empathy. While maintaining professionalism, understanding the perspective of the individuals involved, even if their behavior is unacceptable, can significantly aid in de-

escalation. Recognizing that individuals may be acting out due to stress, intoxication, or other underlying factors, allows for a more compassionate and effective response. This doesn't condone aggressive or disruptive behavior, but it does provide a framework for understanding the root causes and crafting a more tailored approach.

However, empathy should never compromise safety or

security. If verbal de-escalation techniques prove ineffective, or if the situation poses a clear and present danger, security personnel must be prepared to take appropriate action. This may involve requesting backup, utilizing physical restraint techniques (only when absolutely necessary and in accordance with training and legal guidelines), or contacting emergency services. The use of physical force should always be the last resort, and must be proportionate to the threat and justified under the law.

The effective use of physical intervention, when necessary, is a specialized skill requiring extensive training. This includes learning appropriate restraint techniques that minimize the risk of injury to both the individual being restrained and the security personnel. Ongoing training and regular refresher courses are crucial in maintaining proficiency and adherence to best practices. De-escalation training should also cover legal and ethical considerations, ensuring personnel

understand their rights and responsibilities, and the potential legal ramifications of their actions.

Moreover, the effectiveness of conflict resolution and de-escalation is significantly enhanced by a strong team approach. Clear communication channels between security personnel, management, and emergency services are vital. A well-coordinated response, with different team members taking on specific roles, can ensure a swift and effective resolution to even the most challenging situations. Regular team briefings and debriefings after incidents allow for a shared learning experience, identifying what worked well and areas for improvement.

Technology also plays a crucial role. Body-worn cameras can provide valuable evidence in case of disputes or

allegations of misconduct, ensuring accountability for both security personnel and patrons. Furthermore, improved CCTV systems and communication devices allow for quicker response times and better coordination between security personnel. However, technology is only a tool; its effectiveness depends on how it's integrated into a comprehensive security strategy that prioritizes de-escalation and conflict resolution.

The history of security within the night-time economy

reveals a gradual shift from a primarily reactive to a more proactive approach. The focus is increasingly on preventing incidents rather than simply responding to them. This shift demands a greater emphasis on training, particularly in conflict resolution and de-escalation techniques. Investing in comprehensive training programs, ensuring regular updates and refresher courses, and creating a culture of continuous learning are crucial elements of a modern and effective security operation.

Furthermore, the effectiveness of security personnel is

significantly enhanced by a strong working relationship with venue management and local law enforcement. Regular communication, joint training exercises, and shared strategies allow for a coordinated approach to maintaining safety and security. This collaborative approach breaks down silos and fosters a unified front against disorder and crime. It also encourages a better understanding of the challenges faced by each stakeholder, contributing to more effective and informed decision-making.

In conclusion, effective conflict resolution and de-escalation are not merely desirable skills for security personnel within the night-time economy; they are essential components of a robust and proactive security strategy. This requires a multifaceted approach, integrating verbal and non-verbal communication skills, a deep understanding of human behavior, and the willingness to intervene early and appropriately. By prioritizing de-escalation and providing comprehensive training, the night-time economy can create safer and more enjoyable environments for all, fostering a culture of proactive safety and responsibility. The long-term investment in training and development pays significant dividends in reducing incidents, improving public safety, and enhancing the overall reputation of the industry. The

evolving landscape of the night-time economy necessitates a continuous commitment to professional development, ensuring security personnel are equipped with the skills and knowledge to navigate the complexities of their roles and contribute to a safer and more vibrant environment. The future of security hinges on this proactive and preventative approach, transforming the role of security personnel from reactive responders to proactive guardians of public safety.

Effective Crowd Management Strategies for Different Events

The principles of effective crowd management, honed over decades within the security industry, transcend the specific venue. While a bustling nightclub presents unique challenges compared to a large-scale outdoor festival, the underlying strategies share common threads. Successful crowd management hinges on proactive planning, robust communication systems, and a highly trained team capable of adapting to unforeseen circumstances. This is not merely about preventing chaos; it's about creating a safe and enjoyable environment for everyone involved.

One critical element is understanding crowd dynamics. People behave differently in different settings. The energy of a rock concert differs drastically from the more subdued atmosphere of a classical music performance. A security team needs to be acutely aware of these subtle shifts in mood and behavior, anticipating potential flashpoints before they ignite. For instance, bottlenecks at entrances and exits are a classic source of frustration and potential for conflict.

Effective planning necessitates meticulous attention to these choke points, implementing strategies to ensure smooth and efficient crowd flow. This might involve multiple entry and exit points, clearly marked pathways, and well-trained personnel guiding patrons. Signage should be prominent, simple, and universally understandable, regardless of language barriers. Consideration should also be given to the layout of the venue itself; is there sufficient space to accommodate the expected number of attendees comfortably? Are there enough restrooms and refreshment areas to avoid long queues? Overcrowding, even in a well-managed space, can quickly escalate tensions and create an unsafe environment.

Emergency procedures are not merely contingency plans; they are the bedrock of effective crowd management. These plans need to be detailed, regularly rehearsed, and

understood by every member of the security team. Clear communication channels are vital, employing a combination of visual and verbal cues. Designated personnel should be responsible for monitoring crowd density, identifying potential problems, and reporting them promptly to the command center. This might involve the use of radio communication systems, strategically placed surveillance cameras, and regular patrols to ensure all areas of the venue are constantly monitored. Emergency exits should be clearly marked and easily accessible, free from obstructions. Staff training should include drills on evacuation procedures, ensuring a swift and orderly dispersal of the crowd in the event of an incident.

Effective communication extends beyond internal team coordination. It encompasses engaging with the public, proactively addressing potential issues, and fostering a sense of collaboration. Security personnel should be trained to communicate calmly and assertively, defusing tense situations before they escalate. This includes clear and concise instructions, patience, and empathy. A well-trained security professional understands that communication is a two-way street; listening to concerns and addressing them directly can significantly reduce the likelihood of conflict.

For large-scale events, public address systems are

indispensable for announcements, instructions, and

emergency warnings. These systems should be tested rigorously before the event commences to ensure they are functioning correctly and easily understood. Furthermore, the use of social media and other digital platforms can be employed to disseminate information, respond to queries, and proactively address concerns prior to and during the event itself. This proactive communication strategy minimizes uncertainty, keeps the crowd informed, and ultimately enhances the overall experience.

The specific strategies employed will naturally vary

depending on the type of event. A football match demands a different approach than a music festival. For instance, managing the flow of spectators entering and leaving a stadium requires a highly coordinated effort involving numerous security personnel, stewards, and potentially local police. Clear zones need to be established for ticket checking, bag searches, and body checks, minimizing congestion and potential delays. High-risk areas, such as areas where rival supporters might congregate, require a heightened security presence. Moreover, careful planning is needed to manage the movement of large numbers of people towards public transport after the event concludes. In

contrast, a music festival presents its own set of challenges, often involving a significantly larger and more diverse crowd spread across a larger area. The emphasis here might be on perimeter security, managing access points, and addressing potential crowd surges. Effective zoning, clear signage, and easily identifiable support points are critical in this context.

The evolution of technology has significantly impacted crowd management. CCTV systems provide real-time

surveillance, allowing security personnel to monitor crowd density, identify potential problems, and respond quickly to incidents. This technological advancement offers a comprehensive overview of the venue, enhancing situational awareness and enabling proactive intervention. Furthermore, predictive modeling can analyze past data to anticipate potential problems and refine security deployments. The use of facial recognition technology, while raising privacy concerns, can be a powerful tool for identifying and tracking individuals of interest. However, the ethical considerations and potential biases associated with such technology need careful consideration and ethical implementation. The integration of these technologies into the overall crowd management strategy must be meticulously planned and implemented to ensure data privacy and effective usage without infringing on civil liberties.

Beyond technology, the human element remains crucial. The effectiveness of any crowd management strategy ultimately rests on the skills and training of the security personnel involved. Regular training sessions focusing on de-escalation techniques, conflict resolution, and emergency response are essential. This training should encompass both theoretical knowledge and practical exercises, preparing security personnel for a range of scenarios. Simulations and role-playing can be particularly valuable in developing their skills and building confidence. Furthermore, promoting a culture of teamwork and communication within the security team is paramount. Effective collaboration enhances efficiency and ensures a swift and coordinated response to any incident.

The team needs to function seamlessly as a unified force, with each member aware of their roles and responsibilities.

In conclusion, effective crowd management is a multifaceted endeavor, demanding meticulous planning, robust communication, and a highly trained security team.

Understanding crowd dynamics, anticipating potential

problems, and having well-defined emergency procedures are all critical components of a successful strategy. The integration of technology, while enhancing capabilities, cannot replace the human element. The skills and training of security personnel remain paramount, and a culture of

proactive safety and responsibility, coupled with continuous professional development, are essential to ensuring a safe and enjoyable experience for all. The future of crowd management lies not only in technological advancements but also in a holistic approach, emphasizing proactive planning, effective communication, and the well-being of all involved.

Collaboration Between Security and Law Enforcement Agencies

The seamless integration of security personnel and law enforcement agencies is paramount to a safe and secure night-time economy. This collaboration isn't simply about reacting to incidents; it's about proactively shaping a preventative environment. Effective partnerships require clear communication channels, shared training initiatives, and a mutual understanding of each other's roles and

limitations. This synergistic relationship extends beyond simply responding to immediate threats; it delves into intelligence sharing, preventative strategies, and post-incident analysis to continuously improve safety measures.

One crucial aspect of this collaboration is the establishment of robust communication protocols. This goes beyond simple radio contact; it encompasses the establishment of joint operational centers or designated points of contact where information can be rapidly exchanged. For example, in areas with a high concentration of licensed premises, a dedicated liaison officer from the local police force could be embedded with security teams during peak hours. This would facilitate real-time intelligence sharing, allowing for rapid response to potential threats or disturbances. Imagine a situation where a known troublemaker is identified entering a venue; the security team, in liaison with the police officer, can discreetly monitor the individual's behavior, preventing escalation before it occurs. This proactive approach significantly reduces the likelihood of incidents requiring a full-blown police response.

Furthermore, joint training exercises significantly enhance the effectiveness of this collaboration. Scenario-based training, simulating various emergency situations – from crowd crushes to aggressive individuals to potential terrorist threats – allows security personnel and law enforcement officers to practice coordinated responses. These exercises build familiarity and trust between the teams, solidifying communication protocols and refining operational procedures. For instance, a mock active shooter drill could involve security personnel securing the immediate area, guiding patrons to safety, and providing crucial information to responding police officers, such as the location of the shooter and the number of casualties. This shared training promotes a unified response, maximizing efficiency and minimizing casualties during a real-world emergency.

Beyond immediate response, the sharing of intelligence is vital. Security personnel, being on the ground and observing patterns of behavior nightly, possess unique insights into potential threats that might not be readily apparent to law enforcement. This includes identifying individuals with a history of violence, recognizing escalating tensions between groups, or spotting suspicious activities. By establishing secure channels for this information to be relayed to the police, law enforcement can proactively address potential issues before they escalate into incidents. This might involve increased police patrols in specific areas, pre-emptive

interventions with known troublemakers, or enhanced

security measures at vulnerable locations. This collaborative intelligence sharing, often facilitated through secure online platforms or regular briefings, creates a proactive security network, preventing many incidents from ever occurring.

The legal framework supporting this collaboration is also crucial. Clear guidelines outlining the roles and responsibilities of both security personnel and law enforcement must be established and consistently applied. This includes defining the circumstances under which security personnel can legally detain individuals, the

appropriate use of force, and the procedures for handing over suspects to the police. Regular reviews and updates to these guidelines, taking into account evolving legislation and best practices, are essential to maintain legal compliance and ensure a clear understanding of responsibilities. Ambiguity in these matters can lead to misunderstandings, legal challenges, and ultimately, undermine the effectiveness of the collaborative relationship. Clear legal frameworks not only protect both security personnel and law enforcement officers, but also ensure a consistent and effective response to security challenges.

Moreover, the ongoing professional development of both security personnel and law enforcement officers is critical for maintaining a high standard of collaboration. Training programs should incorporate modules on inter-agency cooperation, legal frameworks, communication skills, and de-escalation techniques. Regular refresher courses, coupled with opportunities for joint training exercises, reinforce best practices and ensure that both teams are equipped to handle the evolving challenges of the night-time economy. This shared commitment to ongoing learning promotes a culture of continuous improvement, adapting responses to emerging threats and technological advancements. This continuous professional development ensures the partnership remains robust, adaptable, and effective in the face of evolving challenges.

The success of this collaboration is also intrinsically linked to the overall culture of trust and respect between security personnel and law enforcement. Regular meetings, joint planning sessions, and informal communication channels foster stronger relationships, promoting a sense of mutual understanding and shared purpose. By breaking down barriers and fostering open communication, both teams can build a stronger collaborative bond, maximizing their

collective effectiveness. Building this trust and respect takes time and effort, but it is the foundation upon which effective collaboration is built. Open communication channels, built on mutual respect, are essential for achieving synergy and maximizing effectiveness in preventing incidents and responding efficiently to emergencies.

Beyond the immediate operational aspects, the collaboration extends to the realm of post-incident analysis. Following significant incidents, joint debriefing sessions are essential to identify areas for improvement. By objectively evaluating the response, both security and law enforcement agencies can pinpoint weaknesses in communication, response times, or operational procedures. This collaborative review helps create a cycle of continuous improvement, leading to more effective strategies and a higher level of preparedness for future incidents. The data collected from these post-incident reviews can be used to refine training programs, revise operational guidelines, and implement technological improvements. This continuous learning cycle ensures that the partnership remains effective and efficient in the face of emerging security challenges.

Further enhancing this collaboration is the utilization of modern technology. Shared databases containing information on known offenders, individuals banned from premises, and locations with a high propensity for incidents can significantly improve situational awareness. Real-time crime mapping systems can assist in deploying resources effectively, predicting potential hotspots, and informing proactive policing strategies. Body-worn cameras, utilized by both security personnel and law enforcement, provide valuable evidence in case of disputes or incidents, promoting transparency and accountability. This integration of technology improves information sharing, enhances situational awareness, and streamlines responses, contributing to a safer environment for both security personnel and patrons.

The role of licensing and regulatory bodies is also crucial in supporting this collaboration. The Security Industry

Authority (SIA) in the UK, and similar regulatory bodies in other countries, play a significant role in setting standards for security personnel training, licensing, and professional conduct. By ensuring that security personnel receive appropriate training and are held to high standards of professionalism, regulatory bodies contribute to a more reliable and effective partnership with law enforcement. This includes consistent background checks, regular training updates on relevant legislation and best practices, and a clear complaints procedure to address issues and ensure

accountability. The SIA's involvement not only enhances the professionalism of the security sector but also significantly enhances the reliability and effectiveness of the collaborative relationship with law enforcement. This strengthens trust and ensures consistent standards are adhered to across the sector.

In conclusion, the collaboration between security personnel and law enforcement agencies is not merely desirable; it's essential for maintaining public safety and fostering a secure night-time economy. Through robust communication protocols, joint training exercises, intelligence sharing, clear legal frameworks, continuous professional development, a culture of trust and respect, post-incident analysis, and the strategic use of technology, this partnership can be significantly strengthened. The collective expertise and resources of both sectors, when effectively coordinated, create a proactive and reactive approach to security, maximizing safety and well-being for everyone involved in the night-time economy. The future of night-time security lies in the strengthening and continuous evolution of this vital partnership.

Emerging Threats and Challenges in the NightTime Economy

The night-time economy, a vibrant tapestry of entertainment, social interaction, and economic activity, faces an ever-evolving landscape of threats and challenges. While traditional concerns like public disorder and alcohol-related violence persist, new complexities demand a reassessment of security strategies and personnel training. The rise of

terrorism, for instance, has fundamentally shifted the

security paradigm, demanding a proactive approach that goes beyond simple crowd control and incident response. The vulnerability of large gatherings, particularly in densely populated urban areas, presents a significant challenge, requiring sophisticated risk assessment and preparedness strategies. Security personnel must now be trained not only to manage drunken patrons but also to recognize and respond to potential terrorist threats, including identifying suspicious behavior, coordinating with law enforcement, and implementing emergency evacuation procedures. This necessitates a significant upgrade in training, incorporating counter-terrorism awareness, active shooter response protocols, and enhanced communication systems.

Beyond the threat of terrorism, the digital age presents a new frontier of security concerns in the form of cybercrime. The increasing reliance on digital systems for everything from access control to point-of-sale transactions creates vulnerabilities that can be exploited by criminals. Data breaches, cyberattacks targeting financial systems, and online scams aimed at both businesses and patrons pose significant risks. Security personnel need to be aware of these potential threats and equipped to identify and report suspicious online activity. This might involve monitoring social media for potential threats, recognizing phishing attempts, and reporting cyber incidents to appropriate authorities. The training must extend beyond physical security protocols to incorporate a basic understanding of cybersecurity threats and how to mitigate them.

The evolving social dynamics within society also present unique challenges. The rise of social media has amplified the impact of viral events and online criticism, demanding a more nuanced approach to public relations and crisis management. Security incidents that were once contained within the physical boundaries of a venue can now rapidly escalate into national or even international news stories through online dissemination. Security personnel must be trained to manage the online narrative surrounding incidents, working collaboratively with venue management to respond quickly and effectively to negative publicity. This requires a sophisticated understanding of social media platforms, crisis communication strategies, and the importance of maintaining a positive public image. The ability to de-escalate situations through effective communication, both on-site and online, is becoming increasingly important.

Furthermore, the increasing prevalence of mental health issues presents a complex challenge for security personnel.

Interactions with individuals experiencing mental health crises require a delicate balance between safety and

compassion. Security professionals are increasingly on the front lines of addressing these issues, requiring specialized training in recognizing signs of distress, de-escalating tense situations, and collaborating with mental health professionals to provide appropriate support. This training should emphasize empathy, communication skills, and a comprehensive understanding of mental health issues and best practices for intervention. Moreover, adequate support and resources for security personnel who deal regularly with these challenging situations are crucial to their well-being and effectiveness.

The rise of new technologies presents both opportunities and challenges. While advanced surveillance systems like AI-powered facial recognition and predictive analytics offer potential benefits in terms of crime prevention and resource allocation, they also raise significant ethical concerns about privacy and potential biases. The use of such technologies requires careful consideration of their implications for civil liberties and the establishment of clear guidelines for their ethical implementation. Training should emphasize responsible technology use, awareness of potential biases, and adherence to data privacy regulations. Additionally, the deployment of robots and drones for security purposes presents a new frontier, requiring training on their safe and effective operation as well as the legal and ethical considerations surrounding their use.

The increasing complexity of the night-time economy also necessitates a more integrated approach to security.

Collaboration between security personnel, law enforcement, venue management, and local authorities is essential for effective crime prevention and incident response. This might involve joint training exercises, information sharing, and the development of comprehensive security plans that encompass all stakeholders. Security professionals are no longer simply "bouncers" but key players in a complex ecosystem that requires coordinated effort and communication. The future of security in the night-time economy hinges on the ability of all stakeholders to collaborate effectively.

The future of security in the night-time economy will also require a shift in the perception of security personnel. They are no longer solely reactive enforcers but proactive guardians of public safety and community well-being. Their role is evolving to encompass community engagement, conflict resolution, mental health support, and even crisis communication. This demands a higher level of training, improved professional development opportunities, and recognition of their crucial contribution to the economic and social vitality of the night-time economy. The development of specialized training programs that address the specific challenges and responsibilities of security personnel in the modern context is crucial. This might involve incorporating elements of social work, psychology, and public relations into existing security training curriculums.

Furthermore, the industry must address the issue of worker well-being. The job of a security professional can be stressful, demanding, and often involves exposure to

violence and trauma. Providing adequate support, including mental health services, stress management training, and access to employee assistance programs, is crucial for the physical and mental health of security personnel. Creating a supportive and inclusive work environment will also contribute to attracting and retaining qualified individuals, ultimately enhancing the overall quality of security services.

In summary, the future of security in the night-time economy is characterized by a convergence of emerging threats, technological advancements, and evolving social dynamics.

To navigate this complex landscape, security professionals require advanced training, sophisticated technologies, and a collaborative approach that involves all stakeholders. The emphasis should be on proactive crime prevention, effective conflict resolution, the responsible use of technology, and a commitment to the well-being of both security personnel and the public they serve. The night-time economy's success hinges on the ability of the security industry to adapt, innovate, and rise to these unprecedented challenges. Only then can the vibrant and essential contribution of this sector continue to thrive.

Technological Advancements and Their Impact on Future Security Practices

The integration of technology into security practices within the night-time economy is accelerating at an unprecedented rate. This technological evolution presents both significant opportunities and considerable ethical challenges, demanding careful consideration and proactive planning from all stakeholders. The potential benefits are undeniable, offering the promise of enhanced safety, improved efficiency, and a more proactive approach to crime prevention. However, the potential for misuse and the ethical implications of these powerful tools necessitate a thoughtful and balanced approach.

Artificial intelligence (AI) is poised to revolutionize security operations. AI-powered surveillance systems, for example, can analyze vast amounts of data from CCTV cameras in real-time, identifying potential threats such as suspicious behavior or escalating conflicts far more efficiently than human observers. Facial recognition technology, while controversial, can aid in identifying known troublemakers or individuals who pose a risk to public safety. Predictive policing algorithms, based on historical crime data, can help security personnel deploy resources more effectively to areas with a higher probability of incidents, allowing for a more proactive and preventative approach to security. This data-driven approach allows for the efficient allocation of

resources, enabling quicker response times to incidents and ultimately reducing the risk of violence or disorder.

Furthermore, AI can be integrated into access control

systems, enhancing security at venues by verifying identities and controlling entry. The ability of AI to identify patterns and anomalies in security footage can lead to quicker identification of potential problems, such as a large and unusually fast influx of people to a particular area or sudden changes in crowd behavior. Such early warnings can prevent issues from escalating.

However, the use of AI in security also raises significant ethical concerns. The potential for bias in algorithms,

particularly in facial recognition technology, is a major point of contention. Studies have shown that these systems can be less accurate in identifying individuals from certain ethnic groups, leading to potential misidentification and unfair targeting. Data privacy is another significant concern. The collection and analysis of large amounts of personal data raise serious questions about individual rights and the potential for misuse of information. Transparency and accountability are crucial to mitigate these risks, ensuring that the use of AI in security is ethical and respects fundamental rights. Moreover, the reliance on AI should not diminish the importance of human judgment and intervention. Security personnel need to be trained to critically evaluate the output of AI systems and ensure that human oversight remains an integral part of the security process. The blind faith in algorithms can lead to errors in judgment, and the human element is indispensable for ethical decision-making in complex security situations.

Robotics offers another avenue for technological

advancement in night-time security. Autonomous security robots, equipped with cameras, sensors, and communication systems, can patrol venues and public spaces, detecting potential threats and alerting human security personnel.

These robots can also assist in crowd management,

providing a visible deterrent to potential troublemakers and assisting in directing pedestrian traffic. They can provide a continuous monitoring presence in locations with limited human staffing, offering both a cost-effective and efficient approach to security. Moreover, robots can access and

traverse areas that would be difficult or dangerous for human security personnel, such as narrow alleyways or dimly lit areas. The potential for robots to undertake routine tasks, such as monitoring CCTV footage or conducting patrols, frees up human security personnel to focus on more complex tasks, such as conflict resolution and incident response. This enhanced efficiency can lead to improved response times and better overall security outcomes.

Yet, the deployment of robots in security also faces practical and ethical challenges. The cost of acquiring and

maintaining robotic systems can be substantial, making it an inaccessible technology for smaller venues or businesses.

The technical reliability of the robots and their ability to cope with unforeseen situations also need to be addressed.

Furthermore, the potential for robots to malfunction or be hacked presents a security risk in itself. The use of robots must be carefully integrated into existing security protocols to ensure a seamless and effective operation. Moreover, the ethical considerations related to the use of autonomous robots in security settings require further attention. The use of robots to enforce security measures can create concerns related to human oversight and potential biases in their decision-making algorithms. The issue of accountability for robot actions also needs to be addressed. A clear understanding of the legal and ethical responsibilities associated with robot deployment is crucial for the responsible integration of robotics into night-time security.

Advanced surveillance systems, combining high-definition cameras, advanced analytics, and integrated data management, are becoming increasingly sophisticated. These systems allow for real-time monitoring of large areas, enabling security personnel to identify and respond to incidents quickly and effectively. The use of thermal imaging cameras can assist in detecting individuals hiding in shadows or obscured from view, enhancing situational awareness. The integration of facial recognition technology into these systems, although controversial, can facilitate the identification of known offenders and individuals posing a threat. The use of such integrated technologies enables a holistic approach to security, improving situational

awareness, response capabilities, and overall security

efficacy. However, the ethical considerations surrounding data privacy and potential biases in surveillance systems are critical. The implementation of robust data protection

measures and the establishment of clear guidelines for data usage are vital to ensure the ethical and responsible

deployment of such technology. Furthermore, the

transparency and accountability surrounding data collection and analysis are fundamental for maintaining public trust. The continuous monitoring of surveillance footage must be balanced with respect for individual privacy rights.

Biometric technologies such as fingerprint scanning and iris recognition are also gaining traction in the night-time economy. These systems offer a high degree of accuracy in identifying individuals, providing enhanced security measures for access control and authentication purposes.

They can limit unauthorized access to secure areas within venues and aid in the quick identification of suspected individuals involved in incidents. These technologies contribute to a more secure environment by enhancing the accuracy of verification processes and minimizing the potential for fraud or impersonation. However, the implementation of biometric technology raises concerns about data privacy and security. The potential for data breaches and the misuse of personal biometric information necessitate the establishment of robust security protocols and compliance with relevant data protection regulations. The secure storage and handling of biometric data are paramount, and strict guidelines should be in place to protect individuals' privacy. Public education on the benefits and risks of biometric technologies is vital for gaining trust and ensuring public acceptance.

The future of security in the night-time economy will likely be shaped by a complex interplay of these technological advancements. The successful integration of these technologies depends on a careful balancing act, weighing the benefits of increased security and efficiency against the potential risks to privacy and the need for ethical considerations. The development of robust regulatory frameworks, ethical guidelines, and transparent data governance practices is essential to ensure responsible innovation and prevent the misuse of powerful technologies.

The training of security personnel in the ethical use and limitations of these technologies is also paramount. The ultimate goal is to create a safe and enjoyable night-time economy, harnessing the power of technology while

upholding fundamental human rights and promoting public trust. This involves not just technological advancements but also a shift in mindset, embracing a more proactive, preventative, and data-driven approach to security, while always prioritizing the human element. Security professionals will need to be adaptable, well-trained, and ethically aware to navigate the complex challenges and opportunities presented by the future.

The Role of Data Analytics in Improving Security Outcomes

The transformative potential of data analytics in enhancing security within the night-time economy is undeniable. No longer are security professionals solely reliant on reactive measures; the ability to analyze vast datasets allows for a proactive and predictive approach, moving beyond simply responding to incidents to anticipating and preventing them. This shift represents a fundamental change in the operational philosophy of security, demanding a new skill set and a more data-literate workforce.

One of the most significant applications of data analytics lies in predicting potential incidents. By analyzing historical data on crime patterns, incident reports, weather conditions, and even social media trends, sophisticated algorithms can identify potential hotspots for trouble. Imagine a system that analyzes past incidents of violence outside a specific bar on Friday nights, correlating this data with factors such as the number of patrons, the type of music playing, and even the time of year. Such a system could then predict the likelihood of similar incidents occurring in the future, allowing security personnel to preemptively deploy resources to mitigate the risk. This proactive approach not only enhances safety but also significantly improves the efficiency of resource allocation.

Optimizing resource allocation is another key area where data analytics proves invaluable. Rather than deploying security personnel based on intuition or historical precedent, data-driven insights enable a more strategic and efficient distribution of resources. For instance, by analyzing data on crime rates and incident frequency at different times and locations within a city's night-time economy, security managers can allocate personnel where they are most needed, ensuring optimal coverage and maximizing the effectiveness of their teams. This intelligent allocation not only reduces unnecessary costs but also ensures a more effective response to potential threats.

Furthermore, data analytics offers a powerful tool for evaluating the effectiveness of existing security measures.

By tracking key metrics such as the number of incidents, response times, and the effectiveness of various intervention strategies, security managers can gain valuable insights into what works and what doesn't. This data-driven evaluation allows for continuous improvement and optimization of security protocols, ensuring that strategies remain effective and adapt to evolving challenges. For example, if data reveals that a particular security camera placement is ineffective at deterring crime, it can be adjusted or replaced based on the analytical insights gained. This allows for ongoing refinement of the security infrastructure,

maximizing its overall efficacy.

The implementation of data analytics in the night-time

economy, however, is not without its challenges. Concerns around data privacy and the ethical implications of using personal information are paramount. Security companies must adhere to stringent data protection regulations and ensure that all data collected and analyzed is handled responsibly and ethically. Transparency and accountability are crucial to build and maintain public trust. Individuals need to understand how their data is being used and have the ability to control their personal information. The

development and implementation of robust data governance policies are, therefore, essential to allay these concerns and foster trust amongst the public.

Another significant challenge lies in the need for skilled professionals who can effectively utilize and interpret the data generated by these systems. Security personnel require training and development in data analysis and interpretation, enabling them to understand the insights gleaned from the data and use them to inform their decision-making. This necessitates investment in training programs and educational resources, ensuring a competent and data-literate workforce.

This educational component must also address the ethical considerations involved, ensuring that security professionals are trained not only to use data effectively but also to do so responsibly.

Furthermore, the integration of data analytics systems into existing security infrastructure can be a complex and costly undertaking. The initial investment in software, hardware, and training can be substantial, requiring careful planning and resource allocation. The ongoing maintenance and updating of these systems also present considerable operational costs, demanding sustained investment and commitment. Therefore, a thorough cost-benefit analysis is essential to ensure that the benefits of implementing data analytics outweigh the financial investment involved.

Beyond the technological aspects, the successful

implementation of data analytics hinges on collaboration and information sharing. Security companies, law enforcement agencies, and local authorities must work together to share relevant data and coordinate their efforts. This collaborative approach ensures a holistic and comprehensive understanding of the security landscape, enabling more effective crime prevention and response strategies. Such collaboration also fosters a sense of trust and mutual respect among the involved parties, which is essential for successful implementation.

In conclusion, data analytics presents a transformative opportunity to enhance the security outcomes of the night-time economy. Its ability to predict potential incidents, optimize resource allocation, and evaluate the effectiveness of existing measures is undeniable. However, the successful integration of data analytics necessitates careful consideration of ethical implications, investment in skilled professionals, and robust collaboration among stakeholders.

By addressing the challenges and embracing the

opportunities, the night-time economy can leverage the power of data analytics to create a safer and more enjoyable environment for everyone. The future of security in the night-time economy is not just about more cameras and more guards, it's about smarter strategies, informed decisions, and a proactive approach to maintaining public safety. The potential for improved efficiency, better risk assessment and ultimately, fewer incidents, is too significant to ignore. The challenge now lies in its careful and ethical implementation, ensuring that data becomes an ally, not an adversary, in the ongoing pursuit of a safe and vibrant night-time economy. The responsible use of data analytics represents a significant step forward in ensuring a safer and more enjoyable experience for all those who work and recreate in the night-time economy, enhancing both the safety and the economic viability of this vibrant sector.

The successful integration of data analytics into night-time security strategies will not be achieved overnight. It requires a phased approach, starting with pilot programs to test and refine methodologies, followed by a gradual expansion across wider geographical areas and different sectors of the night-time economy. Careful evaluation of each stage is paramount, allowing for adjustments and improvements based on the insights gained. Continuous professional development for security personnel is also crucial, ensuring they possess the necessary skills and understanding to navigate this evolving technological landscape responsibly and ethically. This ongoing development will not only enhance the effectiveness of security measures but will also build confidence and trust amongst both the public and the workforce. The successful deployment of data analytics in night-time security requires careful planning, robust governance structures, and a commitment to ongoing

learning and development – ensuring that technology serves to enhance safety and not compromise the vital human element at the heart of security operations.

Furthermore, the potential for data analytics extends beyond crime prevention. It can be utilized to monitor and improve the overall efficiency of security operations. By analyzing data on response times, staff deployment, and incident resolution, managers can identify areas for improvement and optimize workflows. This data-driven approach to operational management can lead to significant cost savings and enhanced efficiency, freeing up resources to be allocated to other crucial areas. Moreover, this approach allows for continuous improvement, allowing for refinement based on real-time feedback and performance data. The optimization extends to better understanding patron behavior, allowing venues to better manage crowd flow, anticipate potential issues, and tailor their security strategies accordingly. This integrated approach demonstrates the far-reaching potential of data analytics in transforming not just the safety, but also the overall operational effectiveness of the night-time

economy.

The ethical considerations around data privacy must remain at the forefront of any implementation strategy.

Transparency and accountability are essential to building public trust. This means clear policies regarding data collection, storage, use, and retention must be in place, and these policies must be easily accessible to the public.

Independent audits of data practices should be conducted regularly to ensure compliance with regulations and ethical standards. The public must be confident that their data is being handled responsibly and that their privacy rights are being respected. This builds trust and ensures that the benefits of data analytics are realized without compromising fundamental human rights. The responsible and ethical implementation of data analytics will not only enhance security but also build stronger relationships between the security industry and the communities it serves.

The Future of Security Training and Professional Development

The effective integration of data analytics, as discussed in the previous chapter, necessitates a significant shift in the training and professional development of security personnel within the night-time economy. The security professional of the future will need a skillset far beyond the traditional competencies. Simply possessing a valid SIA licence will no longer suffice; continuous learning and upskilling will be crucial for maintaining professional standards and effectively leveraging technological advancements. This necessitates a fundamental re-evaluation of existing training programs and the creation of new educational pathways designed to equip security professionals with the knowledge and abilities

required to navigate the evolving landscape.

One of the most significant challenges lies in bridging the gap between the theoretical knowledge imparted in training and the practical application of that knowledge in real-world scenarios. Current training often focuses on theoretical aspects of security, including legal frameworks, conflict management techniques, and basic first aid. While essential, these elements must be complemented by a more robust focus on practical skills development through simulation exercises, role-playing, and real-life case studies. This immersive approach would allow trainees to develop critical thinking skills, problem-solving abilities, and decision-making capabilities under pressure, mirroring the demands of the night-time economy environment.

Furthermore, the increasing reliance on technology demands a significant overhaul of training curricula. Security personnel must be equipped to effectively utilize various technological tools, including CCTV systems, access control systems, and data analytics platforms. Training programs must incorporate modules dedicated to technology utilization, data interpretation, and cybersecurity awareness. This should not be limited to simply learning how to operate the technology; it must also include training on the ethical implications of data usage, the importance of data privacy, and the responsible application of technological tools. This understanding is crucial not only for ethical practice but also for ensuring compliance with increasingly stringent data protection regulations. Ignoring this aspect can lead to severe legal and reputational consequences for both individuals and the organizations they work for.

The integration of scenario-based training, using virtual reality (VR) and augmented reality (AR) technologies,

presents an exciting opportunity to enhance the realism and effectiveness of security training. VR and AR simulations can recreate complex and potentially dangerous situations, allowing trainees to practice their responses in a safe and controlled environment. This immersive learning experience can significantly improve decision-making under pressure and enhance situational awareness, skills crucial for effective security operation in the dynamic environment of the night-time economy. For example, trainees could participate in simulated crowd control scenarios, practice de-escalation techniques, or respond to incidents involving aggressive individuals, all within a virtual environment. This reduces the risk of injury to both trainees and instructors while maximizing the learning outcome.

Another crucial aspect of future security training is the incorporation of cultural sensitivity and diversity awareness.

The night-time economy is diverse and multicultural, and security personnel must be equipped to interact effectively and respectfully with individuals from various backgrounds and cultures. Training should address unconscious bias, promote inclusive communication strategies, and equip personnel to handle potentially sensitive situations involving individuals from diverse backgrounds. This training must be ongoing and continually updated to reflect the evolving social landscape.

The development of specialized training pathways, catering to the specific needs of different roles within the security industry, is also essential. For instance, door supervisors in high-volume nightclubs will require different skills and training than those working in smaller pubs or security personnel responsible for monitoring CCTV footage remotely. Tailoring training programs to specific job requirements ensures that individuals receive the most relevant and beneficial education. This targeted approach maximizes the effectiveness of training resources and

ensures that security personnel are adequately equipped to perform their duties effectively.

The future also necessitates a move toward a more

continuous professional development model. Security is a constantly evolving field, with new threats, technologies, and best practices emerging regularly. The SIA licensing requirements represent a significant step, but ongoing

professional development beyond these requirements must be promoted and incentivized. This could involve a points-based system rewarding continued learning and the acquisition of new skills, leading to career progression and enhanced professional standing. Regular refresher courses, advanced training modules, and opportunities for specialized certification in areas such as counter-terrorism, crowd management, or cybersecurity would ensure that security professionals stay at the forefront of their field.

Furthermore, collaboration and knowledge sharing across the security industry should be encouraged. This could involve regular conferences, workshops, and online forums where security professionals can network, share best practices, and learn from each other's experiences. Such collaborative initiatives promote innovation and ensure that the entire sector benefits from advances in security techniques and best practices. Industry-academia partnerships could also play a significant role in developing and delivering cutting-edge training programs that integrate theoretical knowledge with practical application and cutting-edge technologies.

The financial investment in security training and

professional development is paramount to achieving these goals. Government funding, industry contributions, and private investment must all contribute to creating high-quality training programs, providing access to advanced technologies, and supporting the continuous professional development of security personnel. This financial

commitment not only enhances the quality of security services but also contributes to a more robust and safer night-time economy. Incentivizing continuous learning through financial rewards or career advancement opportunities will attract and retain talented individuals, further bolstering the professionalism and effectiveness of the security sector.

Finally, the development of robust evaluation mechanisms to assess the effectiveness of training programs is essential. This includes not only measuring the knowledge and skills acquired by trainees but also evaluating the impact of the training on real-world performance and overall security outcomes. This data-driven approach allows for the continuous improvement of training programs, ensuring that they are meeting the needs of the ever-evolving night-time economy and providing security personnel with the tools they need to excel in their roles. The collection and analysis of this data can inform future curriculum design, identify areas where training needs improvement, and ultimately contribute to a more secure and enjoyable environment for everyone in the night-time economy. By investing in robust training, we can ensure a more professional, skilled, and ethically responsible security workforce, thereby

strengthening the safety and security of the night-time economy for years to come.

The Changing Role of Security Personnel in the NightTime Economy

The preceding chapter highlighted the crucial need for

advanced training and professional development to meet the evolving demands of the night-time economy. This

necessitates a forward-looking perspective, anticipating how the very role of security personnel will transform in the years to come. Several key factors will shape this transformation: shifts in societal attitudes towards security, the relentless march of technological innovation, and the ever-changing landscape of the industry itself.

One significant trend is the growing public awareness of issues like diversity, inclusion, and de-escalation techniques.

The expectation of security personnel is no longer solely focused on physical intervention and conflict resolution. Instead, there's an increasing demand for professionals who can de-escalate tense situations through communication and empathy, fostering a safer and more inclusive environment for all patrons. This requires a fundamental change in training, moving beyond traditional "muscle-first" approaches to prioritize conflict de-escalation, cultural sensitivity, and effective communication strategies. Curricula must incorporate role-playing scenarios that simulate diverse situations, forcing personnel to adapt their responses to

individual circumstances, acknowledging the nuances of human interaction and avoiding generalizations based on appearance or behavior. This shift necessitates a more

nuanced understanding of human psychology and effective communication techniques, including active listening, nonverbal cues recognition, and empathy-driven responses. The successful security officer of tomorrow will be as skilled in diplomacy as in physical intervention.

Technological advancements are also reshaping the industry, creating both challenges and opportunities. The widespread adoption of CCTV systems, facial recognition software, and predictive analytics algorithms offers unprecedented opportunities to improve security and enhance safety.

However, this also necessitates skilled personnel capable of interpreting and effectively utilizing this data. Security personnel will need training in data analysis, cybersecurity, and the ethical implications of using advanced technologies.

The reliance on technology shouldn't overshadow the

importance of human interaction. While technology can provide valuable data and insights, it cannot replace the human element crucial for assessing complex situations, reading body language, and making informed, ethical

decisions in real-time. The ideal scenario involves a

synergistic approach, where human judgment guides the use of technology, rather than technology replacing human intuition. This requires cross-training personnel in both the technological and interpersonal aspects of security. They must be adept at utilizing technological tools while maintaining strong communication and de-escalation skills.

The integration of Artificial Intelligence (AI) presents both exciting opportunities and potential concerns. AI-powered systems could analyze security footage in real-time, identify potential threats, and alert security personnel before incidents escalate. AI-driven predictive policing models might identify high-risk areas or times, allowing for proactive deployment of resources. However, the ethical implications of using AI in security must be carefully considered. Bias in algorithms, privacy concerns, and the potential for misuse are significant challenges that need to be addressed through rigorous ethical guidelines and ongoing oversight. The training of future security professionals must include a thorough understanding of AI technology, its limitations, and its ethical considerations. They must be equipped to critically evaluate the output of AI systems and understand when human intervention is needed. Moreover, a comprehensive understanding of data privacy regulations and ethical decision-making in the context of AI deployment will be critical.

Beyond technological advancements, the very nature of the night-time economy itself is undergoing a transformation.

The rise of the gig economy, the increasing use of online booking platforms, and the changing demographics of

nightlife all have implications for the role of security

personnel. Security needs will shift to accommodate new venue types, such as pop-up bars and event spaces,

demanding flexibility and adaptability from security

professionals. The growing use of cashless transactions will alter the risk landscape, impacting security protocols and training. The increasing popularity of online reviews and social media means that the actions of security personnel will be subject to immediate public scrutiny. This underscores the need for robust training in customer service, conflict resolution, and media relations. Security personnel will need to be skilled communicators, able to address concerns promptly and professionally, both in person and online. This requires comprehensive training programs that address the changing dynamics of reputation management in today's digitally connected world.

The future of security in the night-time economy also hinges on the development of robust professional standards and licensing frameworks. While the Security Industry Authority (SIA) provides a valuable framework, continuous review and modernization are crucial to meet evolving demands. This includes strengthening vetting procedures, implementing stricter standards for training and licensing, and creating more rigorous mechanisms for monitoring and accountability. A more robust system of continuous

professional development (CPD) is needed, ensuring that security personnel maintain their competence and stay

abreast of the latest industry best practices and technological advancements. This could involve mandatory refresher courses, online modules, and opportunities for specialized training in areas such as de-escalation techniques, mental health awareness, and cultural sensitivity.

Furthermore, the industry needs to invest in fostering a

culture of continuous learning and professional development.

Security personnel should be encouraged to participate in ongoing training, share best practices, and engage in

professional networking opportunities. This requires a

concerted effort from industry bodies, training providers, and employers. Incentivizing continuous learning through improved career pathways and opportunities for

advancement will encourage security professionals to invest in their own professional development, ultimately benefiting the entire industry. This also necessitates a shift in the perception of security work, moving away from viewing it as a low-skilled occupation towards recognizing it as a demanding and responsible profession that requires ongoing education and development.

Finally, collaboration between security professionals, law enforcement, local authorities, and venue owners is crucial for creating a safer and more enjoyable night-time economy. Open communication channels and shared intelligence can help prevent incidents, identify emerging threats, and ensure that security resources are deployed effectively. This collaboration could involve joint training exercises, regular information sharing, and the development of joint strategies to address specific security challenges. The aim should be a coordinated approach to security management, leveraging the expertise of all stakeholders to create a comprehensive and effective security system. This approach ensures that security measures are aligned with broader community safety objectives and promote a positive and safe environment for all.

In conclusion, the future role of security personnel in the night-time economy will require a fundamental shift in both skills and mindset. The successful security professional of tomorrow will be a skilled communicator, a technology adept, a culturally sensitive individual, and a responsible professional committed to ongoing learning. By embracing technological advancements responsibly, strengthening professional standards, and fostering collaboration across various stakeholders, the industry can ensure that the night-time economy remains a safe and vibrant space for everyone.

Investing in the training and development of security

personnel is not just a matter of professional advancement; it is an investment in the safety and well-being of communities and the continued success of the night-time economy. The future of security isn't just about preventing incidents; it's about creating a more inclusive, safer and positive experience for all those who enjoy the vibrancy and excitement of the night-time economy.

Acknowledgments

This book would not have been possible without the

generous contributions of many individuals. First and

foremost, I extend my deepest gratitude to the numerous door supervisors, security managers, and SIA-licensed personnel who shared their invaluable experiences, insights, and stories. Their willingness to open up about the challenges and rewards of their profession forms the very heart of this narrative. Their candid accounts bring a much-needed human element to a often overlooked profession.

Finally, I am eternally grateful to Emma for their

unwavering support, patience, and understanding throughout this lengthy undertaking. Their encouragement and belief in this project kept me going, particularly during challenging moments.

Appendix

This appendix contains supplementary materials that provide further context to the information presented in the main body of the book. It includes:

Appendix A: A timeline of key legislation affecting the UK security industry.

This timeline details the key

legislative changes impacting the security industry,

providing a chronological overview of significant legal developments.

Appendix B: Examples of SIA licensing regulations and training requirements.

This section offers illustrative examples of the specific standards and requirements set by the Security Industry Authority, providing a more detailed look at the regulatory landscape.

Appendix C: Statistical data on incidents in the night-time economy.

This section presents relevant statistical data on crime and incidents in the night-time economy, offering a quantitative perspective on the challenges addressed in the book. (Note: Data will be anonymized to protect privacy.)

Glossary

This glossary provides definitions of key terms and concepts used throughout the book, ensuring clarity and

understanding for readers with varying levels of familiarity with the security industry:

Bouncer:

An informal term for a door supervisor or security personnel at a pub or nightclub.

Crowd Control:

Strategies and techniques used to manage and regulate groups of people in public spaces or events.

De-escalation:

Techniques for reducing tension and conflict in potentially volatile situations.

Licensed Door Supervisor:

A security professional holding an SIA license to work in a designated capacity.

Night-Time Economy:

Businesses and activities operating during evening and night hours.

SIA (Security Industry Authority):

The UK regulatory body for the private security industry.

Venue Security:

Security measures implemented within a specific location, such as a pub, nightclub, or event.

Author Biography

Antonio Templar is an SIA Trainer, Door Supervisor

industry professional. With over 24 years of experience. He brings a unique blend of practical insight and academic rigor to this exploration of the security industry. Antonio Templar's personal experience within the security industry, combined with his academic background, provides a compelling perspective on the

historical evolution and cultural dynamics of this often-overlooked profession.

www.ingramcontent.com/pod-product-compliance
Lightning Source LLC
LaVergne TN
LVHW050537160826
845677LV00011B/2075

* 9 7 9 8 2 3 0 5 6 5 0 5 5 *